S1
Design &
Typography

S2
Planning
& Usability

S3
Business
Value

III

Understanding the Principles of Successful Web Site Design

Brian Miller
Foreword by Roger Black

BOOKS

For more excellent books and resources for designers, visit www.MyDesignShop.com.

15 14 13 12 11   5 4 3 2

Distributed in Canada by Fraser Direct
100 Armstrong Avenue
Georgetown, Ontario, Canada L7G 5S4
Tel: (905) 877-4411

Distributed in the U.K. and Europe by F+W Media International
Brunel House, Newton Abbot, Devon, TQ12 4PU, England
Tel.: (+44) 1626-323200, Fax: (+44) 1626-323319
Email: postmaster@davidandcharles.co.uk

Distributed in Australia by Capricorn Link
P.O. Box 704, Windsor, NSW 2756 Australia
Tel.: (02) 4577-3555

Library of Congress Cataloging-in-Publication Data

Miller, Brian D. (Brian Donald), 1973-
Above the Fold / by Brian Miller.—1st ed.
p. cm.
Includes index.
ISBN 978-1-4403-0842-0 (pbk. : alk. paper)
1. Web sites—Design. 2. Web site development. I. Title.
TK5105.888.M553 2011
006.7–dc22
2010013201

Edited by Eve Bohakel Lee, Lee Copywriting
& Editing, Louisville, KY
www.LeeCopywriting.com

Designed and art directed by Brian Miller
Design Group, Norwalk, CT
www.BrianMillerDesign.com

Produced by Crescent Hill Books,
Louisville, KY
www.CrescentHillBooks.com

Every reasonable attempt has been made to identify owners of copyright. Errors or omissions will be corrected in subsequent editions.

For my beautiful wife Bridgette.

Acknowledgements

This book simply would not have been possible without the guidance, support, and valued friendship of my longtime mentor, Alex W. White. There are countless designers whose ability to think and see has been forever impacted by Professor White's articulation of the principles of type, image, and space—but none more grateful than this one.

I owe a special thank you to Nancy Heinonen at Crescent Hill Books for her patient, professional, and informed management of this entire process.

Thank you to Roger Black for lending his valuable time and knowledge to this project.

I also want to acknowledge my fellow Type Directors Club board members, as well as my current and former students, for reminding me of the *real* reasons I pursue a career as a designer.

To Shick, my constant companion.

And, of course, Sarah and Bridgette, with love and gratitude.

Table of Contents

Above the Fold: Foreword by Roger Black
On not starting at the beginning

Web design is always a conflict between the "stakeholders" and the users.

Typically, at the kickoff meeting, all the stakeholders come with a list of their most important requirements for, say, a landing page. If you've got ten in the room, each with a list of five "musts," that's fifty things that the client wants. But a user, coming to the page, just wants one thing. And so the conflict begins.

A designer's job is to pare those things down and put them in a place where users can find them if they want them, and ignore them if they just want to know the price of the ticket, or read the story, or watch the video, or somehow achieve their goal on clicking the link that brought them there.

Many times there is something they don't care about, like advertising, that is essential to the business of the site. The designer may be forced to ignore the end clients, the users, to get paid!

Similarly, there are conventions of Web design (like putting a lot of things on a page) that users have gotten to expect, but they don't help make a page look good. Designers ignore these conventions at their own risk.

Resolving these conflicts aren't always easy, and this book provides a number of tools to help. Brian Miller is first of all a typographer. Since Web pages consist largely of text (in area, if not in file size), learning how to handle type is a key skill for a Web designer. (See Chapter 5.)

As well as abundant common sense, Brian brings his design experience in corporate, retail, and media fields to the Web. His sites have a sophisticated and classical look, one that is very clean, organized, and even elegant. The things he learned in the offline world play a role here. And guess what? Users know these conventions too. Grids and columns, for example, are a familiar organizing principle.

And that's a key underlying principle of *Above the Fold*. Web design does not live on its own planet. It's connected to the rest of the world. Things you've learned from other media and other kinds of design, such as architecture and industrial design, are useful here. Users can latch onto that, when they see it.

So don't start at the beginning. Start with what you know.

Preface

In preparing to write this book, I spoke with several colleagues and asked them what they would find valuable in a book about Web design. One of the most memorable of these discussions was with Jeffrey Kroll, a friend and colleague from my days at Digitas. In typical Jeff fashion, he turned the conversation around and began asking me the questions: "What do you want people to do as a result of reading the book?" he asked. Embarrassingly, I didn't have an answer.

Jeff's question got me thinking about the purpose of the book, and I remembered a story I heard in graduate school. It was the story of a behavioral study that was conducted to see how children would react to an unfenced playground compared to a playground with a fence around the perimeter. Interestingly, the children in the unfenced playground grouped themselves in the center of the unenclosed area, while the children in the fenced playground played and explored all areas of the enclosure.

The conclusion is simple: Rules, represented in this story by the fence, are comforting. They help us feel safe and allow us to explore beyond our comfort zone.

That's what I want this book to be—a comforting fence for anyone interested in exploring the specific nuances of Web design. This book is not about timely design or technology trends; instead, *Above the Fold* is about the timeless fundamentals of effective communication within the context of Web design. It is intended to help you, the reader, understand the "perimeter fences" that Web designers use to develop successful sites.

"All the News
That's Fit to Print"

The New York Times

LATE CITY EDITION

Weather: Rain, warm today; clear tonight. Sunny, pleasant tomorrow. Temp. range: today 80-86; Sunday 71-64. Temp.-Hum. Index yesterday 69. Complete U.S. report on P. 95.

VOL. CXVIII..No.40,721   © 1969 The New York Times Company   NEW YORK, MONDAY, JULY 21, 1969   10 CENTS

MEN WALK ON MOON

ASTRONAUTS LAND ON PLAIN; COLLECT ROCKS, PLANT FLAG

Voice From Moon: 'Eagle Has Landed'

EAGLE (the lunar module): Houston, Tranquility Base here. The Eagle has landed.

HOUSTON: Roger, Tranquility, we copy you on the ground. You've got a bunch of guys about to turn blue. We're breathing again. Thanks a lot.

TRANQUILITY BASE: Thank you.

HOUSTON: You're looking good here.

TRANQUILITY BASE: A very smooth touchdown.

HOUSTON: Eagle, you are stay for T1. [The first step in the lunar operation.] Over.

TRANQUILITY BASE: Roger. Stay for T1.

HOUSTON: Roger and we are you venting the ox.

TRANQUILITY BASE: Roger.

COLUMBIA (the command and service module): How do you read me? Over.

HOUSTON: Columbia, he has landed Tranquility Base. Eagle is at Tranquility. I read you five by. Over.

COLUMBIA: Yes, I heard the whole thing.

HOUSTON: Well, it's a good show.

COLUMBIA: Fantastic.

TRANQUILITY BASE: I'll second that.

APOLLO CONTROL: The next major stay-no stay will be for the T2 event. That is at 21 minutes 26 seconds after initiation of power descent.

COLUMBIA: tp telemetry command reset to re-acquire on high gain.

HOUSTON: Copy. Out.

Neil A. Armstrong moves away from the leg of the landing craft after taking the first step on the surface of the moon

A Powdery Surface Is Closely Explored

By JOHN NOBLE WILFORD
Special to The New York Times

HOUSTON, Monday, July 21—Men have landed and walked on the moon.

Two Americans, astronauts of Apollo 11, steered their fragile four-legged lunar module safely and smoothly to the historic landing yesterday at 4:17:40 P.M., Eastern daylight time.

Neil A. Armstrong, the 38-year-old civilian commander, radioed to earth and the mission control room here:

"Houston, Tranquility Base here. The Eagle has landed."

The first men to reach the moon—Mr. Armstrong and his co-pilot, Col. Edwin E. Aldrin Jr. of the Air Force—brought their ship to rest on a level, rock-strewn plain near the southwestern shore of the arid Sea of Tranquility.

About six and a half hours later, Mr. Armstrong opened the landing craft's hatch, stepped slowly down the ladder and declared as he planted the first human footprint on the lunar crust:

"That's one small step for man, one giant leap for mankind."

His first step on the moon came at 10:56:20 P.M., as a television camera outside the craft transmitted his every move to an awed and excited audience of hundreds of millions of people on earth.

Tentative Steps Test Soil

Mr. Armstrong's initial steps were tentative tests of the lunar soil's firmness and of his ability to move about easily in his bulky white spacesuit and backpacks and under the...

Introduction

I t's difficult to determine, really, the number of times I've assured a client that his or her name, product, ad, or idea will appear "above the fold," but I'm sure it's easily in the hundreds. What's interesting is that the majority of my clients don't ask me to produce anything that can actually be folded. I'm a Web designer, and it's taken me sixteen years to admit that publicly.

The problem with admitting you're a Web designer is that inevitably the person you're talking to has a twelve-year-old niece who designed and produced a Web site over her summer vacation. Most people don't think of Web sites as even needing a designer. "People can make a living doing that?" they say.

In fact, it's true that throughout the history of the Web, non-Web designers have been shaping the aesthetic of the Web landscape. In the early days of the Web, most "designers" weren't designers at all, but technicians focused on pioneering new means of communication. Soon, due mostly to increasing client demand, classically trained print designers began porting their talents over to Web site design, bringing with them many of the design conventions they were accustomed to.

One of these transplanted conventions is the idea of being "above the fold," which is a phrase that comes from the newspaper industry. It refers to the fact that the most important news items of the previous day would need to appear on the upper portion of the front page. Since most papers were folded for shipping, anything at the bottom of the page would not be seen by passersby. The content that appeared above the fold—*BAND PLAYED TILL END*; *WAR! OAHU BOMBED BY JAPANESE PLANES*; *MEN WALK ON MOON*— attracted people and sold newspapers.

Fast forward to the rise of the Internet, where monitor resolution has as much influence over information hierarchy as the fold in a newspaper did. The information that appears in a browser window needs to engage the user in the same way information on the top half of the first page of a newspaper did. Thus, the phrase *above the fold* was adopted by millions of Internet users.

The phrase "above the fold" reminds us that there are both close similarities and vast differences between print and Web design. The principles of space usage, typography, and other elements of effective hierarchical communication are essential to both print and Web design, but the methods of achieving these principles involve different skill sets and considerations for the end user. That's what this book is about—the fundamentals of graphic design and the specific considerations a designer makes for effective Web communication. And it's the reason *Above the Fold* is a fitting title.

The other reason for choosing *Above the Fold* as the title is more metaphorical and has to do with the type of information you'll find within the book. If the information that appears above the fold on a newspaper or Web site is the most important and engaging of its time, the information you'll find in the book *Above the Fold* is too. It is important that Web designers learn, in addition to the necessary technical aspects of digital media, the fundamentals of design that lead to clear communication. This book looks at Web design as a form of graphic communication—a point of difference from most of the other Web design books on the market. Most of the current books on Web design are outdated before they're even printed, because they focus heavily on style and trends. More troubling is the fact that most books depict Web design as a medium whose ultimate expression

The phrase **"above the fold"** reminds us that there are both close similarities and vast differences between print and Web design.

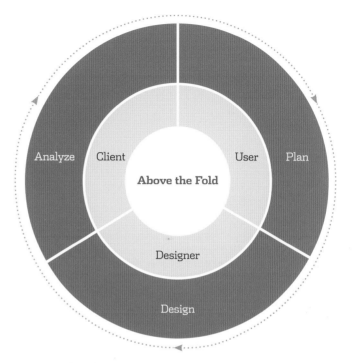

Above the Fold focuses on the three phases of a Web project—planning, design, and analysis—with each phase aligning with the constituents of a Web site: the user, the designer, and the client.

is somewhere between print pieces with movable parts, and movie titles with buttons—more form than substance. The sites in this book put the user first and drive value for the clients they represent.

The majority of the samples chosen to illustrate the concepts in this book are real-world examples produced for clients with strategic business objectives. Designing for clients is significantly more challenging than designing for designers. Portfolio sites and design blogs are often the most beautiful sites on the Web, but being aesthetically pleasing is only one aspect of Web design. *Above the Fold* is divided into three sections: Design & Typography, Planning & Usability, and Business Value. Each section represents a phase in the continuous cycle of Web design. These three sections also neatly align with the players in a Web project—the designer, the target audience, and the client. It's the balance between design, usability, and return on investment that makes a Web site truly great.

Over the past sixteen years of my career, Web designers have gone from being technicians and hobbyists to critical members of the business environment. And for this reason, I'm proud to admit I am a Web designer.

SPENCER AGOSTON, 2010 "UNTITLED"

Connect with *your* MICA. Find information for:

Students · Faculty · Staff · Alumni · Parents · Employers   LOGIN ▾

ONLINE GALLERY
See more current work by students, faculty, and alumni »

M|I|C|A

MARYLAND INSTITUTE COLLEGE OF ART

- About MICA
- Research at MICA
- Admission & Financial Aid
- Programs of Study
- Academic Services & Libraries
- Campus & Student Life

Events & Exhibitions
News
Browse Art
Calendar
Give to MICA

SEARCH

NEWS

LEADING THE WORLD OF VISUAL ART

Joan Waltemath Named Director of Hoffberger School of Painting

THE SECOND-EVER FULLTIME HEAD OF PRESTIGIOUS M.F.A. PROGRAM TAKES REINS AUG. 1

Joan Waltemath will be the second permanent director of the famed Hoffberger School of Painting. Led for more than 40 years by Grace Hartigan until her death in 2008, the M.F.A. program is noted for producing generations of painters who have had an impact in the art world.

Three From MICA Community Receive Notification of Fulbright Scholarships

AWARDS ARE FOR PROPOSALS TO INDIA, TURKEY AND THE CZECH REPUBLIC

Jenny Mullins '09 (Hoffberger School of Painting), Ellyn Stokes '10 (printmaking) and photography faculty member Lynn Silverman have all received notification of winning Fulbright Scholarships for the 2010-11 year.

STUDENT, FACULTY & ALUMNI NEWS

Books, Publications Created by Alumni, Faculty, Students

READING MATERIAL PRODUCED BY THE MICA COMMUNITY

Overview in chronological order of books and articles published or designed by members of the MICA community in 2010. Including, Mina Cheon will read from and sign her book, Shamanism + Cyberspace, May 19 in New York City.

EXPLORING MATERIALS

Two Alumni Compete on New Bravo Series

MARK YOUR CALENDARS: THE FIRST EPISODE OF THIS NEW REALITY COMPETITION AIRS JUNE 9

John Parot '98 and Jaclyn Santos '07 are two of 14 contestants competing in "Work of Art: The Next Great Artist," Bravo's latest incarnation of reality competitions that pits artist against artist.

WATCH

EVENTS & EXHIBITIONS

Commencement Weekend Offers Exhibition, Art Sales, May 13–17

THE WEEKEND INCLUDES THE 2010 COMMENCEMENT EXHIBITION, ARTWALK AND THE MICA MASTERS BENEFIT ART SALE

MICA celebrates its 161st Commencement with a weekend of arts-related events and exhibitions that invite the community to the College.

Contemporary Museum, MICA Organize McCallum and Tarry Survey, May 8–July 31

EXHIBITION PREMIERES THE ARTISTS' 'PROJECTION SERIES' AT THE CONTEMPORARY MUSEUM

LISTEN   WATCH

the first large-scale survey of Bradley McCallum and Jacqueline Tarry, the exhibition premieres the artists' 'Projection Series,' at the Contemporary Museum, May 8–July 31. Earlier site-specific projects will be exhibited throughout Baltimore.

MICA Presents an Exhibition Celebrating the Beauty of Rochefort-en-Terre, May 29–June 20

NINETEEN ARTISTS HIGHLIGHT THE 'MAGIC' OF BRITTANY, FRANCE

MICA presents an exhibition highlighting the work of 19 alumni and faculty who have been inspired by their participation in MICA's celebrated artist-in-residency program. "MICA@Rochefort-en-Terre: MICA Artists, Rochefort Alumni" is on view Saturday, May 29-Sunday, June 20, with a reception on Tuesday, June 8, 5:30-7 p.m., in the Fox Building's Meyerhoff and Decker galleries.

May Boasts Many Off-Campus Exhibitions, Events Featuring Alumni, Faculty, Students

MONTHLY HIGHLIGHTS OF MICA COMMUNITY EXHIBITIONS, INSTALLATIONS

Ongoing list of members of the MICA community who have their work featured in shows, lectures off-campus in May.

M|I|C|A

© 2010 Maryland Institute College of Art

1300 W. Mount Royal Avenue
Baltimore, Maryland 21217
(410) 669-9200

Maps & Directions
Privacy Statement
Contact Us
Students on Our Web Page
Faculty/Staff Directory

WEB DESIGN & TYPOGRAPHY

CHAPTER 1

UNDERSTANDING WEB DESIGN

There's an old legend in the world of football that says Vince Lombardi, head coach of the Green Bay Packers, started every season with a speech to his players about the game of football. He began the lecture by holding up a football and saying, "This is a football." He proceeded to describe its size and shape, talk about how it can be thrown, kicked and carried. Then he'd point down at the field and say, "This is a football field." He'd walk around, describing the dimensions, the shape, the rules, and how the game was played.

This is the Internet

The message from the two-time Super Bowl-winning coach was simple: Remember the basics. This ingenious demonstration stripped away the complexities of the game and reduced it to its essence. In doing this, Mr. Lombardi refocused his players' attention on what was truly important about playing the game of football effectively.

Taking a cue from Vince Lombardi, I'd like to conduct a similar exercise for you: Go over to a computer, open the Web browser of your choice (Safari, Chrome, Firefox, Internet Explorer, etc.), type in the address of your favorite Web site, and behold—this is the Internet. The Internet is a series of interconnected computers, called servers, that enables companies, brands, organizations, governments, religious groups, and individuals to share information on a worldwide scale in real time. The "World Wide Web," or Web for short, is actually only a portion of the Internet, which includes all aspects of computer-to-computer communication like email, messaging and file serving, just to name a few.

When an Internet user types the address of a Web site into his or her Web browser, the computer transmits a signal to a server, and the server responds by sending bits of information back to the computer. This information includes images, raw content, and instructions for the computer to reassemble the layout, called markup (the "M" in "HTML"). The computer then takes that information and configures the files based on two things: the markup and styles that came from the designer/developer, and the preferences and limitations of the Web browser and computer itself. When a computer reassembles a Web page that it has received from a server, the following factors influence exactly how that page appears on the screen:

Color Depth

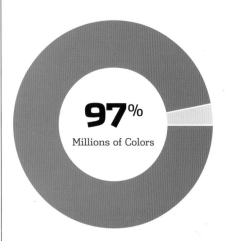

97% Millions of Colors

Color depth is the number of colors that a monitor is able to display. The number depends on the video card in the computer as well as the monitor itself. Most current computers/monitors can display millions of colors, making color-depth a non-issue in most cases of Web design today. In the not-so-distant past, monitors could only display 256 colors. Therefore, Web designers were limited to a color palette of 216 colors called the Web-safe palette. The colors in this palette consisted of the common hues that could be displayed on both Mac and PC operating systems.

Monitor Resolution

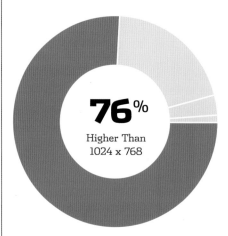

76% Higher Than 1024 x 768

Not to be confused with the monitor size in inches, monitor resolution is the number of pixels when measured horizontally and vertically on a monitor. Most monitors today are 1024 x 768 or higher, although some computers still display at 800 x 600 or even 640 x 480. Most sites these days are optimized for a 1024-pixel width and are designed in a size range of 975 and 990 pixels wide. Fifty or so pixels are subtracted from the overall width to accommodate for the scroll bars and borders on the browser window.

Operating System

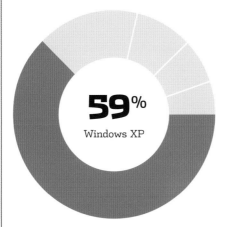

59% Windows XP

The type of computer and version of the operating system (OS) the audience is using to browse a site can have an effect on how a site is seen. The main difference in operating systems is their ability to anti-alias type. Anti-aliased type looks smoother because the system creates a slight blur effect around each character. Non-anti-aliased type can look jagged or "pixelated." The operating system can also limit the availability of certain Web browsers. For example, in 2004, Microsoft suspended development of Internet Explorer for the Macintosh OS because of the emergence of Safari, which is made by Apple.

Browser Type

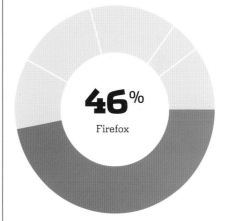

46% Firefox

The primary Web browsers used today are Safari, Chrome, Firefox, and Internet Explorer. A Web browser is an application whose function is to receive layout and styling information from a host and display that information on screen. Because these are different applications developed by different companies, they all interpret this information slightly differently. Added to this, the language that makes up Web styling, cascading style sheets or CSS, is always evolving; therefore, Web browsers are constantly updating to keep up with the latest styling attributes.

While the connection speed of someone browsing a site won't have a direct effect on how a site looks, it will definitely have an effect on the person's experience of the site. This was a major consideration for Web designers in the early days of dial-up Internet—using a phone line to access the Internet. For a time this issue subsided due to the prevalence of high-speed Internet services such as cable and DSL; however, now the issue is re-emerging as a factor in Web design because of mobile Web browsing. Mobile devices are increasingly accounting for a larger percentage of the Web audience, and the majority of mobile browsers use low-bandwidth methods to connect to the Web.

To complicate matters, beyond these inherent system-based influences, individual user preferences also can affect the way a site looks. In this image we see the "Content" preferences in Firefox. These controls allow a savvy Web user to change the fonts, the minimum size for type (this is an accessibility feature for users with impaired vision), the colors used for links, and even whether links are underlined. In some cases, these user preferences can even override the design decisions a designer has made for a page.

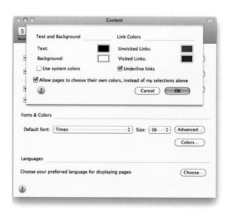

This screenshot of the preferences panel in Firefox shows how users can change how specific characteristics of Web design appear on their screen.

It's this aspect of disassembling a design and allowing the user to reassemble it under a varying set of circumstances that makes Web design unique and challenging.

Limiting **subjective decisions** and
being creative within those limitations
is the essence of what all designers do.

Designing for the Web

To explore the subject of design for any medium, it's important to define the term *design*. At its most basic, design is a plan. Things that are said to have happened "by design" are said to have happened not by accident. So, the more that things appear to have been done on purpose, the more effective a design is likely to be.

A design plan is a series of decisions made by a designer to create a final piece. Clear and defendable decision-making leads to more effective design. Designers are always looking to limit the decisions they need to make in a design, because each decision that's made leaves room for subjective criticism. For example, if a designer chooses to use red as the dominant color of a layout simply because he or she prefers that color, the designer will likely face criticism from a client who prefers any color other than red. However, if the color decision is made for a designer, either by brand guidelines or thoughtful research, the defense of the color is made easier when questioned by a client. Limiting subjective decisions and being creative within those limitations is the essence of what all designers do.

The Web as a design medium comes with several built-in design decision limitations. Designers accustomed to designing for print might be used to controlling things like font selection from a library of thousands of fonts, exact color matching, specific page size and breaks, text wraps, and the use of white space to separate sections of content. In Web design, these luxuries are difficult at best and impossible at worst.

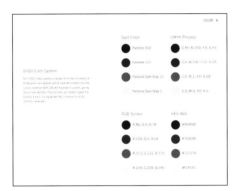

Most organizations have Web standards like this one from the Shintaro Akatsu School of Design (SASD). They spell out the dos and don'ts of everything from typography and color to image use and grid structure. These rules help define the creative decisions made by a Web designer and ensure brand consistency.

Up until very recently, a designer had a choice of only a handful of fonts to choose from for the text on a Web site with only bold and italic styles. Choosing a font for a Web layout meant picking from the small list of fonts that were available on the majority of computers used by the audience of the site. This restriction of Web design, however, is changing rapidly (see Chapter 5, "Web typography").

Design is about having a plan. Web design is about having a **backup plan.**

Color matching is nearly impossible due to the fact that everyone's monitors, graphics cards, and lighting environments are different. Web designers must be tolerant of a range of color matching as opposed to a need for exactness that can be achieved in print. Colors on the Web are made up of the additive spectrum (red, blue, and green—RGB), meaning that all three create white when added together. This is different than with the printing process, which is a subtractive process made up of cyan, magenta, yellow, and black—CMYK. (K stands for black.) When added together these colors create black. Although RGB generally has a wider range of hues—the electric, bright colors—converting design elements from CMYK to RGB when preparing them for the Web can result in slight color shifts that Web designers should be mindful of.

There is no page height or width on the Web. Depending on the length, the content on a Web page can scroll practically forever. This can get overwhelming to a reader and can be dealt with by "paging" the content. A list of Google search results is an example of this.

Pictured here is a single page from Wikipedia.org—the definition of "the Internet." On the Web there is no page height, so pages can go on virtually forever.

Widows, a single word on a line at the end of a paragraph and a typographic no-no, are impossible to predict since the size of type can vary from user to user.

Images on the Web are rectangular only and cannot be rotated. Designers get around this by adding in background color or transparency behind a rotated image. The use of imagery on the Web can be restricted by a target audience's tolerance for download time. The more imagery a page has, the longer it takes to download. As mentioned earlier, this concern waned in the past few years because of the ubiquity of broadband Internet connections, but it is once again becoming a major consideration due to the emergence of mobile browsing.

A Word About the Other Kinds of Sites

There are, of course, ways around the limitations that come with Web design. Using images of type instead of live text, for example, will allow you to have complete control over the type on your site. There are two main issues with this workaround: one, images take longer to download than text, so the more images you have the longer your page will take to load; and two, search engines can't read the content of an image and therefore your search engine ranking can be hurt by this. See Chapter 5, "Web Typography," for more on this subject.

Another means of circumventing Web design limitations is to use alternate development tools such as Adobe Flash or Microsoft Silverlight, which allow a designer to create highly interactive sites that stand independent from standard Web design restrictions—as long as the browser has the correct plug-in. And although Flash has the ability to be search engine-friendly there are very few sites that take advantage of these techniques. There's no doubt that many beautiful and effective Web sites are created using these tools; however, posting images or movies on the Web is a subject for a different book.

Current technologies like JavaScript, Ajax, @fontface and CSS3 can mimic most of the functions that designers used to have to rely on Flash or Silverlight for. Animations, drop-down menus, custom fonts and fades can all now be achieved using native, SEO-friendly text, and simple Javascript code.

The ideal solution is one where each technology is employed to execute that which it is best at. Flash for elaborate 3D animation elements; Ajax or Javascript for key SEO items like navigation; images for imagery and illustration; and native text for the content.

ADOBE FLASH can create extremely dynamic animations and interactivity, but is best used as an element on a page rather than an entire site.

MICROSOFT SILVERLIGHT is similar to Flash in that it can create dynamic elements for a Web site as well as a wealth of back-end functionality.

atf atf

200-POINT GEORGIA
Designed in 1996 by Matthew Carter
(hinted for optimal screen viewing by
Tom Rickner) specifically for the Web

200-POINT TIMES ROMAN
Designed in 1931 by Stanley Morison
and Victor Lardent (Monotype) for
the *Times* newspaper

COUNTERS
The larger counters
on Georgia increase
legibility

X-HEIGHT
Notice the difference
in x-height at the
same type size

CAP HEIGHT
Even the height of
the capital letters
differ at the same
point size

BASELINE
The line on which
letters sit and the
starting point when
measuring the x-height
and cap height

POINTS & PIXELS
The most common unit of measure
when dealing with type is points
and picas. There are 72 points in
.996 inches and standard screen
resolution is 72 pixels per inch (PPI).
Therefore, one point is equal to one
pixel when referencing elements at
screen resolution.

*The x-height, represented by the blue line, is the distance between the
baseline—where the letters sit—and the top of a lowercase letter. It's clear
to see that Georgia, designed by Matthew Carter specifically for the Web,
has a higher x-height than Times Roman at the same size. A counter is the
"hole" created in letters like a lowercase a. In Georgia, the counters are
larger and more open. These characteristics combine to make Georgia more
legible that other serif typefaces when viewed on screen.*

The typographically expressive work of David Carson, like this spread from Raygun Magazine, would be difficult if not impossible to reproduce online without the use of images of type. Outlined type, custom fonts, and type wrapping on a curve are some of the limitations of Web design.

Unlike print layout programs that allow designers to wrap text around a curve, Web design does not yet have such a feature. Text runs in straight columns, aligned to the left, right, or justified. A Web designer's options for using white space to break up large columns of text are reduced to line spacing between paragraphs exclusively. There is no easy method of creating tabbed paragraphs in Web design. French spacing—the use of two spaces after a sentence—is also not possible, since HTML renders any number of spaces as a single space.

Successful Web designers embrace these limitations and find ways to be creative within— instead of trying to circumvent—them. In addition to having a plan, Web designers need to have a contingency plan—a backup plan that allows for user variables. For example, when specifying fonts for live text on a site, a designer will list a series of fonts starting with a first choice, followed by similar font choices in the case the user does not have the first choice:

font-family = Georgia, [if you don't have that then use] "Times New Roman", [if you don't have that then use] Times, [if you don't have that, please just give me something with a...] serif;

When specifying typefaces for Web design, a designer must list his or her preferences for fonts in descending order to accommodate users who don't have the first choice installed on their computer.

Although subtle, the difference in one serif font to another can have a big impact on the overall texture of a design. It's a major component for a designer to have limited control over, but this is rapidly changing, see Chapter 5, "Web Typography."

Napster.com, a peer-to-peer file sharing Web site, launches

Microsoft releases Internet Explorer version 5, which allowed users to save Web pages for the first time

Craigslist.org expands beyond San Francisco (originally launched in 1995)

Google Adwords launches

Netscape version 6 is released

Wikipedia.org launches

Microsoft releases Internet Explorer version 6, which included support for CSS

Google.com, founded by Larry Page and Sergey Brin, launches

Friendster.com launches

Netscape version 7 is released

1998   **1999**   **2000**   **2001**   **2002**

MySpace.com launches

WordPress blogging software is introduced.

Apple releases the Safari Web browser

Facebook.com launches

Flickr.com launches

Mozilla Firefox Web browser is released, which utilizes the Gecko layout engine to display Web pages

YouTube.com launches

launches

Microsoft releases Internet Explorer version 7, which introduced tabbed browsing and a content feed reader

Mozilla Firefox version 2 is released with tabbed browsing

Apple introduces the iPhone and mobile apps

Netscape Navigator version 9 is released

2003   **2004**   **2005**   **2006**   **2007**

points about Web design: The evolution of the Web browser has had a profound impact on Web design, from the use of type to the structure and layout of pages; and Web design is an interactive and evolving process, where "first-to-market" status is more important than design perfection.

Another interesting fact that emerges from this timeline is the evolution of the purposes of Web sites, from serving the company to serving the user. Over time, sites have become utilities that perform functions for the user, not only the organization who builds them.

Good Web Design is an Experience

Good Web design goes well beyond evidence of a plan—good Web design is an experience for the user. The best Web design creates an environment where users feel they have just enough control over the experience that they feel empowered, but not so much control that they feel overwhelmed.

Designing the experience that's right for the target customer is critical to being a successful Web designer. It's the criteria by which each of the samples shown in this book has been judged. It's also the criteria that the Web-browsing population uses to determine how successful a Web site will be.

Take twitter.com, for example. It's unlikely to win a design award, yet it's undeniably and profoundly popular. Twitter's popularity is due largely to two main things: It's a simple idea—telling your friends what you're up to—executed simply with no bells, whistles, or decoration—and users have enough control over the experience to make them feel as if they're expressing themselves—but, again, not so much control that the experience becomes overwhelming or intimidating. Specifically, users can customize their backgrounds and a few colors on the page, but they don't have to be Web designers to achieve something unique.

(Right) Celebrities, companies, and individuals all use Twitter to express themselves by customizing their pages. The Twitter brand itself becomes one of variability.

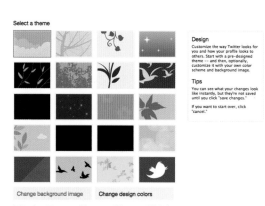

The simple design controls on Twitter give users the experience of "designing" their page without being overwhelmed with too many options.

CHAPTER 2

ANATOMY OF A WEB PAGE

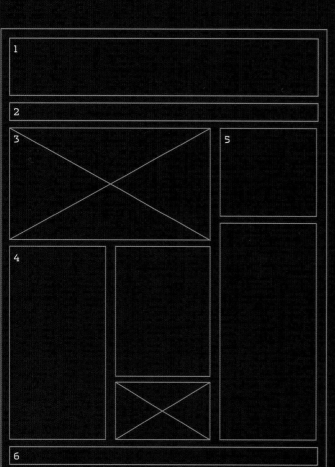

1. Header
2. Navigation
3. Feature
4. Body/Content
5. Sidebar
6. Footer
7. Background

27

Form and Function of Web Design

Web design, as with any other form of design, requires the designer understands the end user's habits, the context in which the work is received and the necessary function of the end result. These factors usually present limitations that set the boundaries for starting design project. For Web design, these boundaries have caused several design and structural conventions to emerge. Such conventions include a page header; persistent navigation; content areas and sidebars; footer navigation; and often a background treatment. Although styling and aesthetics vary greatly from site to site, most sites adhere to this basic structure. Each of these common Web design elements and their placement on the page, came to be for several basic reasons:

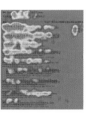

These images show the results of an eye-tracking study. They indicate that users focus their attention on the upper-left area of a Web page.

THE NATURE OF HOW THE PAGES ARE VIEWED.
In Western culture, we're conditioned to read from left to right, top to bottom. Therefore, the natural position for important information would be the upper left of a Web page. This ensures that elements such as logos, navigation and "featured items" are perceived first by the user.

The notion that users scan pages from left to right, top to bottom has been validated through the use of eye tracking studies. Sophisticated cameras fixed to the top of a computer screen have the ability to track the eye movements of Internet users and map out the patterns. The red areas in the images below indicate where users focused most of their attention. They reveal not only the fact that users' attention is mainly focused on the upper left of a page, but also that Web users skim a page for key points, as shown by the spotty bits of color in the center and left image.

Many Web design conventions are borrowed from the world of print communication. Pictured here is the New York Times newspaper showing a header and feature area very similar to those on a Web page.

The "fold"

BORROWED CONVENTIONS.

Because almost all early Web designers were amateur designers or trained as print designers, elements from print design were converted to Web design. Design elements like headers, feature areas, body text, and sidebars all come directly from age-old newspaper design standards.

The "fold" of a newspaper is literally the horizontal crease in the center of the front page delineating the top half from the bottom half. Newspaper editors tend to put as much of the most important information as possible above that fold since that's the area that potential newspaper buyers will see. Similarly, a "fold" on a Web page is the line that delineates where the browser window cuts off the content. Areas above the fold are seen by the user when the page loads. Content below the fold requires that users scroll down.

USER EXPECTATIONS.

Sites that want to attract the masses, like news portals, travel sites, e-commerce sites, etc., need to appeal to the lowest common denominator in terms of one's ability to use technology. As the Web became established in the mid- to late 1990s, companies interested in having their users find what they wanted quickly would imitate the metaphors for navigation and site layout from other, already established, sites. For example, Amazon.com is credited with creating the first tab-style navigation (another borrowed convention); although there are probably earlier examples, the "tabs" served as a metaphor that worked in part because tabs were something people understood from the "real world" of file folders. As a result, Web sites all over the Internet began using a tab structure for their navigation—and still do to this day. Even Apple.com, known widely for its innovative design, once used a tabbed navigation very similar to that of Amazon.

Image of Apple.com from 2007 showing the tabbed navigation style.

At the height of the tab craze in 2000, some said that the navigation on Amazon.com resembled a graveyard.

Search engine optimization (SEO).

Having a high search engine rank is critical to a company's online success. A higher rank on a list of search results means more traffic. Search engines, such as Google.com and Bing.com, use various methods to evaluate the content of a site and determine its rank. Some design factors that influence the search engine optimization of a page include: text links in the main navigation; multiple keyword-rich text links throughout the page; limited use of images, especially images of text, since search engines cannot get content from images; bolded subhead copy styled with the <H> tags; and important content placed above the fold—the higher the better. Although these are not all of the SEO factors that influence the rank of a page, these are generally the factors that a designer has the most control over. The topic of SEO is discussed further in Chapter 8.

Orbitz.com is a good example of a page designed for SEO. Multiple keyword-rich text links, bolded subheads and limited use of imagery consistently produce a top ranking for searches of "Vacation Packages."

ADVERTISING STANDARDS.

The Interactive Advertising Bureau (IAB) was established in 1996 to set up standard practices in Web advertising. The organization sets forth rules that govern the size, shape, and file weight (among other things) for advertising assets. This helps advertisers create a finite series of banners that can be used on any Web site that adopts the IAB standards. For Web designers, this means that their Web design must accommodate banners that are 300 x 250 pixels ("big box"), 180 x 600 pixels ("skyscraper"), and/or 728 x 90 pixels ("leaderboard"), among others. If a Web site is funded with ad revenue, these dimensions become a critical part of the framework of the site. Additionally, advertisers want their ads above the fold so that the user sees them immediately. Web site owners, on the other hand, don't want the ads to overpower the message of their site. Web designers satisfy both sides by establishing a structure that flows with the required sizes of the ads—a 300-pixel-wide sidebar will fit a big box ad without any dead space around it, for example.

Yahoo.com and many other sites across the Web display advertising. In this example of the home page, a "big box" ad appears in the right-hand sidebar. The sidebar for this page has been designed to accommodate banner having a standard width of 300 pixels.

Without **understanding the function** behind standard Web design conventions, designers are purely imitating things that they've seen.

While these particular factors are unique to Web design, the idea of a set of parameters that restricts and informs a design is not unique. Car designers, for example, are faced with hundreds, if not thousands, of these types of challenges. People want to be able to drive more than one make of car without having to work to relocate and decipher the speedometer, for instance. Yet, there's a wide range of variation in the sizes and shapes of cars on the road today.

The duality of form and function is a universal design concept; however, most new Web designers aren't as aware as they should be of the technical and functional implications behind the design decisions they make. Without understanding the function behind standard Web design conventions, designers are purely imitating things that they've seen. This chapter explores the parts of a Web page and specifically how those parts contribute to the overall effectiveness of a site—aesthetically and technically.

Car designers face similar challenges as Web designers when designing a dashboard interface. They seek a balance between unique style and standardization and ease of use.

Beyond Conventional

This chapter examines the structural design conventions that have evolved to make up Web pages. This idea is different than the concept of design templates or "themes" that have become very common with the emergence of content management systems (CMS) like WordPress and Drupal. Below are the "Church Theme" and the "Lifestyle Theme" designed by StudioPress for use with WordPress. Notice how they are identical in structure and format. The only difference between the two is their "skin"—the colors, fonts, and images. While theme-based Web design makes having a Web site easy and affordable, the concept has the potential to erode the value of what Web designers do. At worst, it turns design and creativity into a commodity and homogenizes the look of the Web.

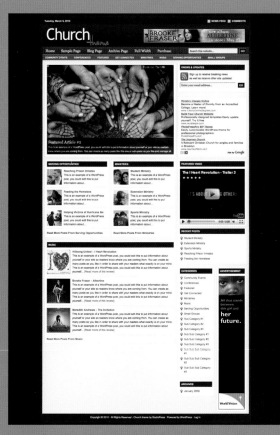

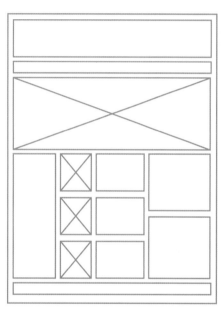

MarthaStewart.com is an elegant design example from both a structural as well as an aesthetic point of view. The subtle and consistent design treatments give the site a uniquely Martha Stewart feel, despite using a standard Web structure.

Header

The header of a Web page is one area that remains relatively consistent throughout a Web site. It acts as a grounding force for the user by identifying and visually unifying all the pages of a site. Headers establish the brand look and feel for a site and often will present the user with a call to action—search, buy, register, etc. The header of a page must perform these tasks without overpowering the content of the page and distracting the user.

The code behind the header contains information that is vital to the search engine optimization of the page. From meta data (keywords and descriptions of the page in the code) to the page title (this is the line of copy that appears on the top of a browser window), search engines use these elements to begin indexing the content of the page.

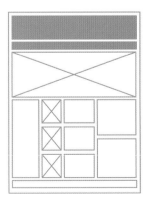

The header graphic for GQ.com uses the magazine's iconic logo as the central element. The clean, centered design approach creates a unique and identifiable presence for the brand.

Headers act as a grounding force for the user by **identifying** and **visually unifying** all the pages of a site.

The header often contains the main navigation for a site. Since navigation is essential for a site's usability, it's logical that it would be placed prominently above the fold. The topic of navigation is explored further in Chapter 7, Planning & Usability.

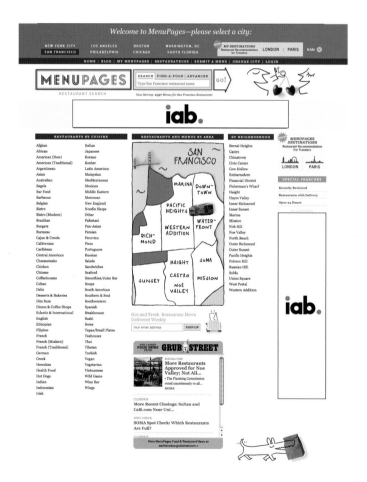

The header for MenuPages.com integrates navigation, branding, a call to action, and advertising space into a delightfully clean and clear presentation.

CNN.com's bold use of their brand color and centered placement of their logo make for a distinctive page header.

WhiteHouse.gov uses a simple and elegant treatment for the header/navigation of the site, with subtle hints of depth and texture.

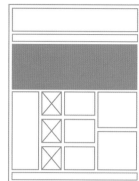

Feature Area

One indication of effective design is a clearly defined hierarchy of information. To achieve this, designers use a focal point—an area in the composition that is perceived before all others and serves as an entry point into the layout. In Web design this is often the main feature area. This area usually takes up a large portion of the home page, has the most vibrant color and typography, and usually features some sort of motion or animation. All of these things combine to make it the most important visual item on the page.

The most common option for a feature area is a slideshow of imagery and content from the site. This can be achieved using SEO-friendly technology like JavaScript and Ajax. Adobe Flash can also be used for highly interactive feature areas or ones that involve sophisticated animation.

MarthaStewart.com has a tasteful feature slideshow that highlights various content from the site with each frame indicated by a tab at the bottom. This solution also includes a pause/play button so users can stop the animation, reducing distractions as they read other content on the page.

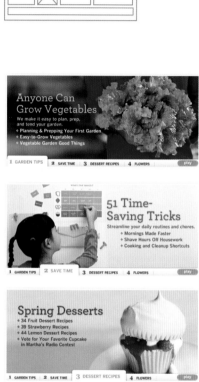

To achieve hierarchy, designers use a **focal point**—an area in the composition that is perceived before all others.

Apple.com uses the feature area to highlight their latest products. Dramatic photos combined with simple, pithy headlines set in minimalist typography result in an impactful presentation with a clear focal point and call to action.

The world's thinnest notebook. **MacBook** Air.

FamousCookies.com uses Flash animation for the main feature. The oversized cookies and type are munched away and replaced one at a time. The combination of HTML and Flash technology works well for this site since the animation serves as an accent for the page, and does not contain any important content that would be hidden from most search engines.

The Winter version of TNVacation.com uses an accordion-style JavaScript feature section. Each "fold" of the accordion contains content pertaining to an area of the site.

BuiltByBuffalo.com, one of the few design agency sites in this book, has a simple yet dynamic feature area on the home page. The photography used in this example overlaps the header area, helping to unify the page and add a sense of depth.

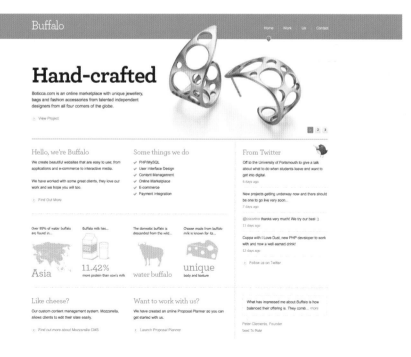

Breaks in the content allow users to scan the layout quickly and gives them **multiple entry points** into the page.

Body/Content

The body or content area of a Web site is where users spend most of their time, as it usually represents the end of their search for content. This is where traditional design ideas of legibility and clarity come into play, but with some added considerations. A Web page can be any height; therefore, it's important to break up long stretches of content with white space and subheadings. These breaks in the content allow users to skim the page quickly, and it gives them multiple entry points into the content.

Dividing up the content by using heading tags (<H1>, <H2>, and so on) helps search engines evaluate the content of a page. Some search engines place a higher value on words contained within these tags, since they tend to summarize the key points from the content.

Bolded subheads, iconography, and generous white space make this page from Apple.com easy to scan to find the information you're looking for.

Energy Efficiency

iMac is designed to be energy efficient right out of the box. It has even earned the EPA's ENERGY STAR qualification for its low power consumption.

Efficient power supply.
iMac includes a highly efficient power supply that reduces the amount of power wasted when bringing electricity from the wall to your computer. Lower power consumption reduces energy bills and lessens the environmental impact of greenhouse gas emissions from power plants.

Advanced power management.
Unlike a lot of Windows–based PC systems, iMac uses energy-efficient hardware components that work hand in hand with the operating system to conserve power. Mac OS X spins down hard drives and activates sleep mode on already energy-efficient LED–backlit displays. And it balances tasks across both central processors and graphics processors. Mac OS X never misses a power-saving opportunity, no matter how small. It even regulates the processor between keystrokes, reducing power between the letters you type. That's just one of many ways Apple manages small amounts of power that add up to big savings.

ENERGY STAR qualification.
iMac meets the stringent low power requirements set by the EPA, giving it ENERGY STAR qualification. ENERGY STAR 5.0 sets significantly higher efficiency limits for power supplies and aggressive limits for the computer's typical annual power consumption.

Eliminating Toxic Substances

It's what iMac doesn't have that makes it more environmentally friendly. It's free of many harmful toxins, including mercury, arsenic, BFRs, and PVC.

Fewer toxins.
The greatest environmental challenge facing the computer industry is the presence of arsenic, brominated flame retardants (BFRs), mercury, phthalates, and polyvinyl chloride (PVC) in products. Apple engineers have worked hard to eliminate BFRs and PVC from iMac circuit boards, internal and external cables, connectors, insulators, adhesives, and more. [2] And they've eliminated many other toxins that are a common part of desktop computer manufacturing — choosing, for example, mercury-free backlighting and arsenic-free glass for the iMac display.

Recyclability

Because iMac is made from materials such as aluminum and glass, it's more likely to be recycled and reused at the end of its long, productive life.

Recyclable materials.
Apple designers and engineers have integrated the entire iMac computer into an enclosure made from a single, solid piece of recyclable aluminum. The display is made of recyclable glass. Both the aluminum and glass materials are very desirable to recyclers, which means the raw materials used in iMac can be reused in other products.

Free recycling for your old computer.
If you live in the U.S., Apple offers a free recycling program for old computers and displays with the purchase of any new Mac. Learn more on the Apple Recycling site.

EPEAT Gold

iMac has earned EPEAT Gold status for its responsible manufacture, energy efficiency, and recyclability.

The EPEAT Gold rating.
Through its innovative and environmentally friendly design, iMac has earned the highest rating of EPEAT Gold[2]. The Electronic Product Environmental Assessment Tool, or EPEAT, evaluates the environmental impact of a product based on how recyclable it is, how much energy it uses, and how it's designed and manufactured.

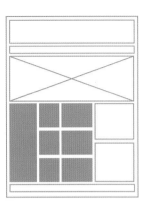

Linked words within the text of a page help to organize ideas and reduce the need for long pages; if a user would like to know more about a related topic, the user can click to another page rather than have all the information on a single page.

Highlighted text links on both GapersBlock. com and AndyRutledge. com help the user scan for related information and key ideas contained within the linked text.

The **optimal line length** for ideal legibility is no more than two to two and a half alphabets—52 to 65 characters.

In addition to not having a height limit, Web pages also don't have a limit to how wide they can be. Web designers have two options for addressing the problem of page width variability. Most current sites have a fixed width frame or boundary, whereas the content is confined to a box with a set size that floats in the browser window as it expands and contracts. The second option is to have variable-width columns. Variable-width layouts were popular in early Web design primarily because they were easy to produce. Designers would simply flow copy into a layout, unconcerned with the consequences of expanding browser windows. The issue with variable width layouts is that without limits to the the length of a line of text, it can become illegible. Typographically, the optimal line length for ideal legibility is no more than two to two and a half alphabets—52 to 65 characters. This prevents eye fatigue both with lines that are too long where a user might lose their place, or lines that are too short where the user is continually going to the next line after just a word or two.

Jaded zombies
acted quietly but
kept driving their
oxen forward.

These three examples of text show how a short line length (top) and a long line length (bottom) make text difficult to consume quickly. The middle example contains 52 to 65 characters in a single line, presenting optimal legibility.

Jaded zombies acted quietly but kept driving their oxen forward. The wizard quickly jinxed the gnomes before they vaporized. All questions asked by five watched experts amaze the judge. Six boys guzzled cheap raw plum vodka quite joyfully.

Jaded zombies acted quietly but kept driving their oxen forward. The wizard quickly jinxed the gnomes before they vaporized. All questions asked by five watched experts amaze the judge. Six boys guzzled cheap raw plum vodka quite joyfully. Just keep examining every low bid quoted for zinc etchings. Sixty zippers were quickly picked from the woven jute bag. Few black taxis drive up major roads on quiet hazy nights. Six big devils from Japan quickly forgot how to waltz. Painful zombies quickly watch a jinxed graveyard.

Wikipedia.org uses a variable width for the body/content area of the page. Both of these images are of the same page, showing a narrow browser window and a very wide window.

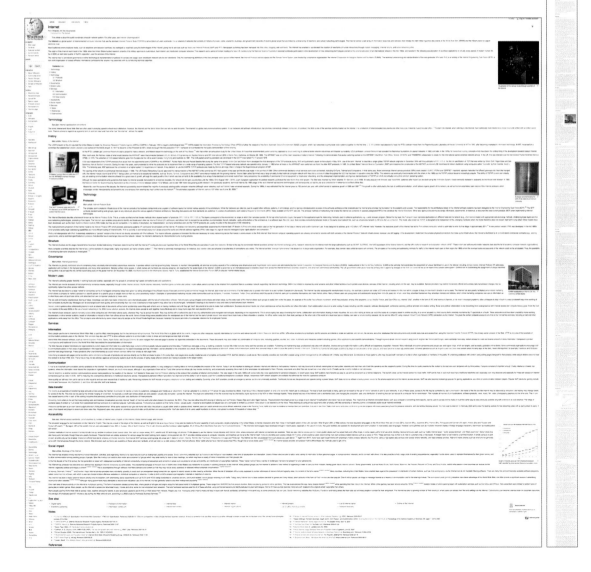

Sidebar

The sidebar of a Web page contains secondary information that either supports the main content of the page or directs users to related content through the use of submenus and links. Areas of a sidebar are often sold for advertising space. Skyscrapers and big boxes typically fit well within the modular structure of a sidebar. As with the header, the design of a sidebar should blend in with the look of the site as not to visually overshadow the content of the page, helping to create an overall feel for the page.

Sidebars, like the ones shown here from Kinder-Aktuell.de (above) and Breez.com.au (right), are useful for providing supporting information as well as advertising space.

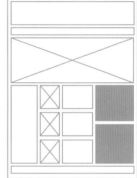

The sidebar on Vimeo.com begins with a call to action for new users to sign up. The 300-pixel-wide column also has space for standard IAB ads and related item links, each color coded for increased usability.

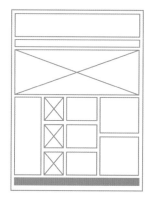

Footer

The footer has emerged over recent years as a critical part of Web design, performing tasks for both the user and search engine optimization. In the early days of Web design the footer would contain the copyright information for the site as well as a couple of links. Over time, Web page footers have grown to resemble a mini site map, with links to each of the main pages of the site. These links not only help the user navigate the site but also help search engines like Google index the site properly, improving the search engine ranking—Google places a higher value on words contained within links.

Technically, the footer of a Web site contains much of the specialized coding for the page like page tracking code or lengthy JavaScript functions. This is again due to SEO. Long bits of copy at the top of a page will push the important information down farther. Google places a higher value on information that's higher up on a page.

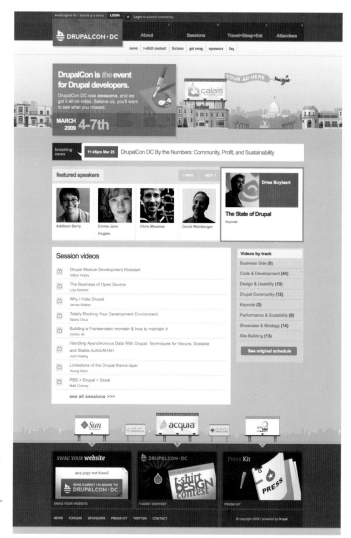

The playful footer of Drupalcon.com provides a tasteful place for sponsor logos and promotional banners in addition to text-based navigation.

*The footer of automaker Honda.com gives a complete
list of areas of the site and also adds a small bit of visual
interest with a randomly appearing image.*

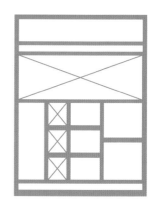

Background

In the earliest days of Web design, designers would use a repeating graphic in the background of a Web page, imitating the effect of patterned wallpaper. Today, Web page backgrounds are used in more sophisticated ways to complement the content of the page. Backgrounds can be used to create depth or dimension, add richness with texture and color to a page, or even expand the content beyond the borders of the page.

The designers of Vaseline.com turned the background into a critical element of the page. Large images of smooth skin lay beneath a simple, CSS design structure.

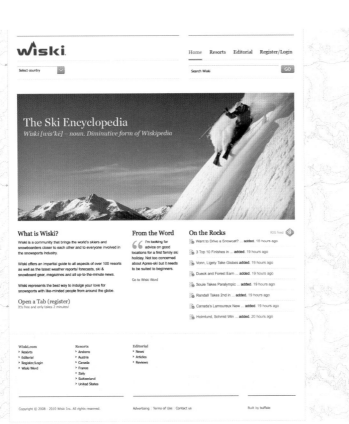

Wiski.com uses a topographical map in the background, which also gives the user a feeling of snow.

TENNESSEE

ABOUT TENNESSEE | CAREERS | PRESS | ▶▶▶ Custom Search | FIND

THINGS TO DO | REGIONS & CITIES | EVENT CALENDAR | PLACES TO STAY | TRAVEL TOOLS | MULTIMEDIA | TRAVEL PROFESSIONALS

LANGUAGE

GET A FREE 2010 VACATION GUIDE
OR VIEW THE E-GUIDE

Map | Satellite | Hybrid

VACATION GUIDE
Request a free vacation guide or view our e-guide version in seconds.

EXPLORE TN
This ticket entitles the bearer to explore the many things to do in Tennessee

01 MUSIC & ARTS
02 FOOD & WINE
03 ATTRACTIONS
04 SPORTS & RECREATION
05 HISTORY & HERITAGE
06 AGRITOURISM
07 NATURE & OUTDOORS
08 SHOPPING
09 SEASONAL SPLENDOR

DISCOVER
READ THE BLOG
TENNESSEE

PREPLANNED TRIP
Watch the slideshow to see a preplanned trip suggestion.

Attractions for Kids
Duration: *as long as you can stay*
Kids of all ages will enjoy frolicking on Tennessee's attractions. With family-oriented fun across...

TENNESSEE'S LATEST
Check out the latest and greatest from around the Volunteer State. Features are updated weekly and provide a quick look at all the most recent happenings from East to West!

FEATURES | ITINERARIES

Weather Alert
The first two days of May brought record-breaking rains to Nashville and surrounding areas in Tennessee. But we want you to know that the show goes on, as Tennesseans have banded together and risen to the occasion, helping both neighbors and strangers. Possibly most inspiring, the Grand Ole Opry, the world's longest running live radio show that has only had to cancel once in it's 85 year history, held a show in its former home, the War Memorial Building, just two days after the flooding. This American treasure that lost so much is as inspiration and an example of spirit that you can experience in our state. Visit »

Springtime in Tennessee
Come out of hibernation! Take a deep breath and enjoy a green Tennessee spring. Visit »

Discover Tennessee Trails & Byways
Behold the backroads. Explore local gems to discover what lies behind and between Tennessee's cities. Visit »

SIGN UP & RECEIVE THE NEWSLETTER
DO YOURSELF A FAVOR. GET THE LATEST NEWS AND BE THE FIRST TO KNOW ABOUT DEALS & CONTESTS.

CLICK TO SIGN UP

⟡ DISCOVER TENNESSEE ⟡
TRAILS & BYWAYS

Take a journey into Tennessee's rich history and heritage on the Old Tennessee Trail. Over eighty points of interest take you from...

CLICK TO CONTINUE

May 2010

SU	MO	TU	WE	TH	FR	SA
						01
02	03	04	05	06	07	08
09	10	11	12	13	14	15
16	17	18	19	20	21	22
23	24	25	26	27	28	29
30	31					

start date ___ and date ___ find

◄ UPCOMING EVENTS ►
Date: May 15, 2010
Free Day in May
Location: *Murfreesboro, TN*
LEARN MORE | SEND INVITE

Date: May 15, 2010
Kitchen & Cookbook Tour
Location: *Bolivar, TN*
LEARN MORE | SEND INVITE

Date: May 15, 2010
Racks by the Tracks Festival
Location: *Kingsport, TN*
LEARN MORE | SEND INVITE

Date: May 15, 2010
Strawberry Festival
Location: *Union, TN*
LEARN MORE | SEND INVITE

Date: May 15, 2010
Strawberry Weekend
Location: *Rutledge, TN*
LEARN MORE | SEND INVITE

See a full listing of our events on the Calendar Page →

Featured Advertising

facebook
FANS OF TENNESSEE

Tennessee on Facebook
👍 Like

27,644 people like Tennessee

Wendy | Olivia | Finalist

Facebook social plugin

twitter
TENNESSEE TWEETS

Stop by the #Chattanooga Visitors Center today & Celebrate Nat'l Tourism Wk w/ free #Moon Pies & #Coke products! (via @chattanoogafun) your cc

Happy Friday! (via @tennesseeshgdd) your cc

Follow TNVacation »

► WATCH VIDEOS ◄

CHECK OUT OUR NEW TV SPOT

TV Spots
Keith Urban TV Spot

THINGS TO DO
Music & Arts
Attractions
Sports & Recreation
History & Heritage
Agritourism
Nature & Outdoors
Shopping
Sustainable Travel

SEASONAL
Spring in Tennessee
Summer in Tennessee
Fall in Tennessee
Winter in Tennessee
Preplanned Trips

TRAVEL TOOLS
Downloadable Maps
Welcome Centers
Air Travel
Road Conditions
Make Contact

MULTIMEDIA
Video Clips
Slideshows
Vacation eGuides
Interactive Vignettes
Wallpapers
Sendable eCards
Downloadable Docs

TRAVEL PROFESSIONALS
Group Travel
Student Tours
Play Tennessee
Meetings & Conventions
Industry Partners
Sustainable Tourism

The background of a Web page doesn't need to recede or be subordinate, as seen in this example from TNVacation.com. The illustration in the background of this home page adds both visual interest and content to the page.

The background images on en.opera.se give a dramatic sense to the pages of the site because of their contrast of scale.

The dark wood panel pattern in the background of VaelProject.com gives the pages texture and creates a mood that's dark, rugged, natural, and masculine.

There is some debate between Web designers and usability experts regarding the use of dark background and light text. Most experts believe that it's more difficult to read light text that's reversed out of a dark background; however, many designers prefer the look of dark backgrounds. As with many other decisions a Web designer makes, this one comes down to the tolerance and preference of their user.

Draplin.com, the Web site for graphic designer Aaron Draplin, offers users the ability to switch from a light to dark background.

Blackle.com, a Web site that employs the Google Custom Search tool, mimics Google.com but with a black background. The site, created by Heap Media, claims to save energy by reducing the amount of watts a monitor needs to display black versus white.

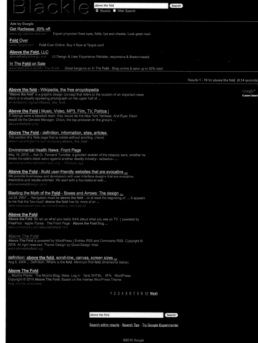

CHAPTER 3

WEB DESIGN UNITY

Until now, this book has been about what makes Web design unique—the special considerations one must make as a Web designer. There are, however, many commonalities between Web design and other forms of communication design—the fundamental principles of organizing space and hierarchical communication that are essential to all forms of design. This chapter explores means of organizing space to enhance a user's access to, and understanding of, information.

Organization and Hierarchy

An effective **design system** takes precedence over the individual elements, so that the user perceives a cohesive unit.

One of the most important aspects of design is the concept of hierarchy. Visual hierarchy is the sequencing of elements within a design. This sequence clearly defines the most important elements of the design, followed by the second most important elements, and so on. Almost every type of information can be broken down into three to four levels of importance. More than that makes contrasting the difference between the levels difficult.

To create hierarchy, a designer must first create a system. A system is created by logically grouping the elements of a design, either through meaning or function, and forming visual relationships between them. An effective design system takes precedence over the individual elements so that the user perceives a cohesive unit. Any element that breaks this system will have more visual value and be understood to have more importance than the other elements, creating a hierarchy.

There are, of course, other methods of developing design systems to create hierarchy. Elements of style such as size, scale, color, texture, and depth are examined in the next chapter, "Elements of Web Design." This chapter focuses on the use of space and the effects of a grid system on Web design.

For example, in a classroom where the desks are neatly arranged in five rows of five desks and each student is sitting in his or her seat, the students appear as a single unit. Regardless of the different genders, clothing, hair styles, or body types, all the students fit within the group because of their organization or spatial relationship to one another. If a single student decided to break the system of rows by moving his desk into the aisle, he would stand apart from the system and give himself visual importance over the other students. The students appear as a single unit because of their arrangement in space—the rows of desks—and the student whose desk is not in line with the others stands out strictly because of his lack of relationship, or his contrast, with the others.

White Space

Creating a design system almost always starts with the clear organization of space. Deliberately constructed white space, not to be confused with unconsidered or empty space, is often overlooked as an element of Web design. In fact, a common mistake among inexperienced designers is to focus too heavily on the "objects" in a design (type, images, points, lines, and planes), and space is simply what's left over when they're finished. Space is essential for creating relationships that form systems that lead to hierarchy.

The interplay between the objects of a design and the background is called the figure-ground relationship. White space, also called negative space, is a reference to the "ground" in "figure-ground." The goal of a designer is to achieve a balance between figure and ground, where one doesn't completely dominate the other. Instead, they work together to unify the design.

White space design elements include:

Margins	the area surrounding a design
Gutters	the space between columns of a grid
Padding	the area around an element contained by a border
Line Spacing	also known as leading, this is the space from baseline to cap height between lines of text
Paragraph Spacing	adding line space is the most common form of paragraph indication in Web design although it is possible to use other methods like indenting, which is also another form of white space

These elements are arranged with no consideration of the space within the layout.

The same elements as above are now grouped and the space has been more clearly defined and organized.

The organization of the space in the layout creates a natural hierarchy or sequence of importance by either relating or separating elements.

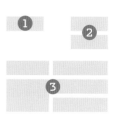

The Gestalt Principles of Perception:
"The whole is greater than the sum of the parts."

Theories involving the psychology of visual organization within art and design come mostly from the Gestalt Principles of Perception. These principles, developed in the early twentieth century at the Staatliches Bauhaus in Germany, refer to the mind's ability to group elements based on one of the following relationships:

SIMILARITY
Grouping of elements that have a unique visual relationship. The two rows of squares above are grouped, despite being separated by a row of circles. The relationship of shape takes precedence over the spacial relationships.

PROXIMITY
Grouping of elements that are close to one another. Two groups are perceived above, despite the fact that there are sixteen individual boxes.

CLOSURE
Grouping of elements that complete a larger unit. A single square is perceived in the above illustration, despite several of the smaller units being removed. The small square in the upper right "closes" the spacing to create a single form.

CONTINUANCE
Grouping of elements that complete a pattern or progression. Each row of boxes above forms a group despite the gaps in the row.

Deliberately constructed white space,
not to be confused with leftover, unconsidered, or empty space, is often overlooked as a useful element of Web design.

InformationArchitects.jp (opposite) uses a minimalist design that relies heavily on the use of white space to organize information and create hierarchy. The gutters, line spacing, and paragraph spacing are carefully crafted to help the user identify individual groups of information.

Similarly, JonTangerine.com (this page) uses wide margins and ample padding to make the page design scannable. With the exception of a small dot of yellow and a bit of red at the bottom, this black-and-white layout uses only a single font (Georgia) yet it has a clear hierarchy of information and plenty of visual interest.

The use of hierarchy and white space in Web design has a bit of extra significance over other forms of communication, since the elements of a design aren't just elements, they're the interface that the user needs to navigate and find information. The primary navigation bar, for example, needs to be immediately identifiable as such, so that the user can navigate the site. The design conventions discussed in the previous chapter help the user identify specific areas of a Web site, but they shouldn't be taken for granted. Guiding the user through a layout should be done deliberately to ensure maximum usability.

This example, from CarterDigital.com.au, uses white space to break up segments of content and lead the user down the page. Items are separated mainly through the use of added space and they're connected by the lack of space, as in the area with the photos.

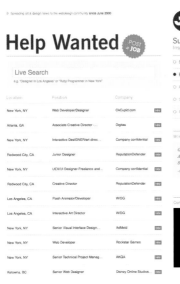

Surfstation.com has long been known for its beautiful design. The latest incarnation of the site emphasizes white space for clear separation of elements and organization.

White space is also essential for making a layout scannable, a critical aspect of Web design. Layouts with well-managed white space allow users to scan information and groups of information to find what they're looking for quickly. Cluttered layouts, or ones that don't effectively manage white space, make it hard for the user to identify patterns which are essential for scanning information. Imagine a group of people milling around at a party versus a line of soldiers at roll call. The people are the same, but the space between them has been organized.

This is a side-by-side comparison of a competition mini-site created by the AIGA DC. On the left is the original site; on the right the white space has been filled in to highlight the consistent and almost rhythmical use of space. The generous spacing around the headline and lead-in statement helps them stand out on the page. The non-default, slightly open line spacing for all the text gives the pages a very light and scannable feel.

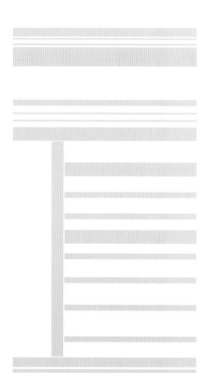

White space is actually a reference to "ground" as in "figure-ground," and doesn't need to be white at all. In this example, ThinkingForALiving.com, the ground is a pink hue, but the result of well-constructed white space on the design is the same.

Containment

At times, more than space is needed to highlight, group, or separate elements on a page. Borders, lines, and boxes can be helpful in defining the space and containing elements within sub-groups. The varying types of borders that can be created with CSS, including dotted, dashed, double, and single lines, make them powerful stylistic elements as well. Even rounded corners, a popular design treatment for boxes, are now possible using CSS3, and they are viewable in browsers compatible with CSS3.

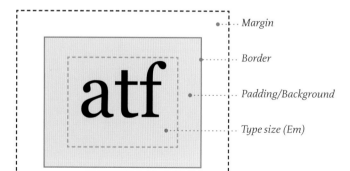

Margin

Border

Padding/Background

Type size (Em)

(Left) CSS can be used to define the border of an object. The border, represented by the orange line in this diagram, lies between the padding distance and the margin area.

*The sites seen here, BrandNew.UnderConsideration.
com (left, top), 20x200.com (left, bottom), and
DollarDreadful.com (above), use a wide variety of
distinctive line styles to segment the page and reinforce
a design style.*

Grids not only organize the elements of a design, they organize the **space** within a design.

Grids

One of the oldest ways to create a balance of figure and ground is through the use of a grid system. Grids not only organize the elements of a design, they organize the space within a design. Clearly aligning design elements through the use of columns creates defined space, and it's this space that gives the appearance of organization.

Early Web sites were laid out using tables, a word processing convention of rows and columns used to arrange elements. Some early Web layouts had a compartmentalized or checkerboard feel as a result of using or overusing tables. Tables are also limited in their flexibility and result in long markup for even simple layouts. Although tables still exist in HTML, <div> or divider tags have taken over as the preferred method of containing and laying out elements of a design. The flexibility of CSS-styled <div> tags more closely resembles the feel of a print layout program such as Adobe InDesign. They enable very sophisticated, print-like layout and grid use.

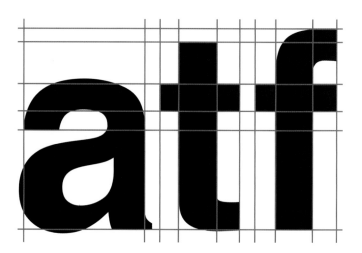

The letterforms of Helvetica, the ubiquitous Swiss typeface and subject of a documentary film, are based on a grid system, making it instantly recognizable over its predecessor, Akzidenz Grotesque.

Neue Grafik
New Graphic Design
Graphisme actuel

Internationale Zeitschrift für Grafik
und verwandte Gebiete
Text dreisprachig
(deutsch, englisch, französisch)

International Review of Graphic
Design and related subjects
Issued in German, English and French

Revue internationale du graphisme et
des domaines annexes
Parution en langue allemande,
anglaise et française

16

Herausgeber und Redaktion
Editors and Managing Editors
Editeurs et rédaction

Druck Verlag
Printing/Publishing
Imprimerie Edition

Richard P. Lohse SWB/VSG, Zürich
J. Müller-Brockmann SWB/VSG, Zürich
Hans Neuburg SWB/VSG, Zürich
Carlo L. Vivarelli SWB/VSG, Zürich

Walter-Verlag AG, Olten
Schweiz/Switzerland/Suisse

New Graphic Design *magazine was started
in 1958 by Richard Paul Lahose, Josef Müllerbockmann, Hans Neuburg, and Carlo Vivarelle.*

*The cover of issue 16, pictured here, illustrates the
grid system that permeated the entire magazine
and is credited with defining the Swiss style of
graphic design.*

CRW / CORPORATE RISK WATCH

Profile
who we are

Services
what we can do

Case Studies
problem solutions

Regions
where we operate

Contact
enquire here

Due Diligence

An international oil company was considering entering into a business relationship with an oil and gas producer in the Philippines but suspected that the target company was associated with local politically exposed persons and that this association might have favoured the company in obtaining a concession for oil extraction. To comply with the Foreign Corruption Practices Act regulations it was necessary to conduct an extensive due diligence to assess the potential risks attached to the deal.

A systematic analysis of publicly available documentation in the Philippines and discreet source enquiries into the target company and its principals were conducted.

It emerged that the management of the oil producer in the Philippines was composed of highly experienced and prominent figures from the public energy sector who continued to retain significant political influence. The beneficial owner of the company in the Philippines was hiding behind nominees and offshore structures but his identity was revealed through discreet enquiries with sources in the local energy sector. It emerged that the ultimate beneficial owner was a former representative of the local government and that his political influence enabled the company to obtain the said concession. The risks attached to the target company were assessed.

Competitor Intelligence

A British company operating in the IT sector was interested in the purchase of one of its three Italian competitors but was unable to put in place the right strategy without having an in-depth knowledge of the Italian IT sector and specifically, the three target companies. In addition the client suspected that one of the players had links to the Organised Crime but was unable to assess the veracity of this rumour.

The work conducted included analysis of the financial situation, business models, investments, marketing and product strategies with respect to each of the three companies through a systematic retrieval, analysis and cross examination of publicly available information, combined with discreet source enquiries with local industry experts.

The work resulted in the identification of one of the tree competitors as the potential acquisition target. Evidence was obtained confirming the allegation of association with organised crime by one of the target companies.

Litigation Support

A Dutch operator in the printing sector suspected that a former employer, an engineer who had worked for the company for over twenty years and who had recently retired, was providing a competitor with the company's know how and other confidential data such as supplier and client contacts. To get these activities to stop, the Dutch operator initiated a legal proceedings against the competitor and its former employees but did not have sufficient evidence to prove the case.

The work conducted consisted in collecting evidence, both factual and testimonial in support to the client's claim, including surveillance and witness identification.

The client was able prove with factual evidence the case of unfair competition. The competitor stopped to act unfairly and the client received compensation for the damages suffered.

Left Loft, the designers of CorporateRiskWatch.com, actually expose the grid structure they're using by tracing it with dotted lines. The elements of every page seem to dance around this five-column grid.

CRW / CORPORATE RISK WATCH

Profile	Services	Case Studies	Regions	Contact
who we are	what we can do	problem solutions	where we operate	enquire here

An in-depth knowledge of business environments and dynamics, persons and companies involved in the business dealings, helps to mitigate risks and to maximise the business opportunities.

Particularly today, the increasingly globalized economy, the rapid growth of the Russian, Chinese and Indian economy and the expansion of the European Union is a double-edged sword for the business as it has opened the door to new markets and opportunities but also to new risks and challenges. Clients are exposed to risks due to a lack of knowledge of new partners, business practices and of the specificities of the business environments in which they operate.

CRW offers business intelligence and financial investigation services to financial institutions, companies and international law firms.

Financial institutions	Companies	Private Equity and Hedge Funds	International Law Firms
1. Due Diligence / Compliance 2. anti-money Laundering	1. Due Diligence / Compliance 2. Competitive Intelligence 3. Financial and Fraud Investigation	1. Due Diligence / Compliance	1. Litigation Support 2. anti-money Laundering

---

CRW / CORPORATE RISK WATCH

Profile	Services	Case Studies	Regions	Contact
who we are	what we can do	problem solutions	where we operate	enquire here

- 1. Why Us
- 2. Mission
- 3. People
- 4. Publications

...olutions help clients mitigate ...he areas of compliance, business ...on, legal disputes and ...ion.

CRW relies on a multi-lingual and highly qualified team and a network of contracted associates worldwide.	CRW provides services to private and public entities, in support of their business activities in Europe, Asia and other regions of the world.	CRW puts particular emphasis on confidentiality, quality and client satisfaction and meets the highest ethical standards.

CRW / CORPORATE RISK WATCH

Profile	Services	Case Studies	Regions	Contact
who we are	what we can do	problem solutions	where we operate	enquire here

CRW relies on a multi-lingual team with international experience in risk management and on a network of contracted professionals worldwide.

The success of our clients' businesses is influenced by decisions taken with respect to new partnerships, investments and business dealings.

CRW's skilled team of multi-lingual team with international experience helps clients mitigate the exposure to financial and reputational risks.

CRW provides clients with reliable information and strategic analysis they require to maximise business opportunities in different regions of the world.

CRW offers services to comply with anti-corruption and anti-money laundering legislations and in support of business partnerships, investments and market entries, hiring of employees, complicated business transactions and legal disputes.

Memberships

Corporate Risk Watch is the holder of a private investigations license, in accordance with the paragraph 134 T.U.L.P.S. issued by the Italian authorities.

Corporate Risk Watch is a member of the following associations:

Association of anti-money Laundering Specialists (www.acams.org)
Italian-American Chamber of Commerce in Italy (www.amcham.it)
Italian-Chinese Chamber of Commerce in Italy (www.china-italy.it)

CRW / ...RATE RISK WATCH

Profile	Services	Case Studies	Regions	Contact
who we are	what we can do	problem solutions	where we operate	enquire here

CRW's s... help clients mitigate risks in t... of compliance, business transacti... disputes and competi...

- 1. Due Diligence and Compliance
- 2. Financial Fraud Investigation
- 3. Competitive Intelligence
- 4. Litigation Support
- 5. Intellectual Property Protection
- 6. anti-money Laundering

CRW is a dynamic, quality oriented risk management and strategic advisory firm.	CRW provides services to private and public entities, in support of their business activities in Europe, Asia and other regions of the world.	CRW puts particular emphasis on confidentiality, quality and client satisfaction and meets the highest ethical standards.

*BlackEstate.co.nz, which has won numerous awards for
its use of typography and unique navigation, features a
six-column grid. The tall page is held together because of
the strict adherence to the elegant grid.*

The Swiss styling of WilsonMinor.com is a classic example of a well-used grid structure. Headlines, subheads, images, and text work together to define and span the six-column grid.

The grid on DigitalPodge.com is filled in a more organic way. Instead of the elements neatly aligning in exactly the same way, there's a playful bouncing of text and image within the grid structure.

To create a fixed-width grid for the Web, a designer must first determine the width of the design, which is determined by the target user's monitor resolution. Most sites are still optimized for 1024 pixels x 768 pixels, therefore most Web grids are between 950 pixels and 990 pixels wide. The reason the width is 25 to 50 pixels less than the monitor resolution is to accommodate for browser elements like scroll bars and window frames, avoiding side scrolling. Once the width has been determined, a designer decides how many columns are needed. Generally, three columns is too limiting, and more columns means more design flexibility; however, too many columns can make recognizing relationships difficult. There is no right number of columns, but the optimal grid gives a layout a clear sense of organization while still allowing for flexibility. The column width for a grid is determined by the overall width divided by the number of columns. And finally, gutters, or the spaces between the columns, are added, providing separation between the elements in each column.

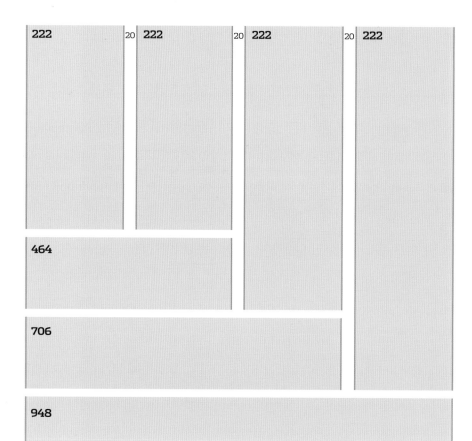

This is a diagram of a grid system with the following specifications:
Width: 948px
Columns: 4
Column width: 222px
Gutter width: 20px
2-col span: 464px
3-col span: 706px

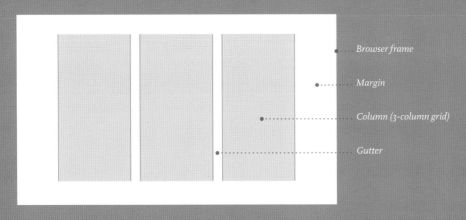

.... *Browser frame*

...... *Margin*

.... *Column (3-column grid)*

.... *Gutter*

FIXED WIDTH (Floating Centered; Fixed Left)

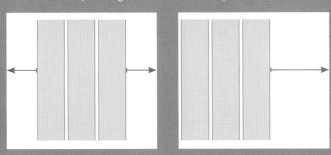

Grids used for Web design need to have a flexible quality to them in order to accommodate varying monitor widths and resolutions. There are several solutions to this issue. In this example of a fixed-width grid, the grid either floats in the center of the browser window or is fixed to the left side. As the browser window expands in both cases, the layout within the grid is not altered.

VARIABLE WIDTH

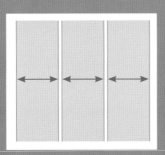

In a variable-width grid system, each column expands proportionately with the width of the browser frame. This causes the layout within the grid to change and shift depending on the width of the user's monitor.

COMBINATION OF VARIABLE AND FIXED WIDTH

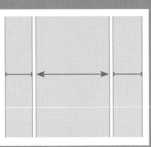

This diagram shows a grid that has both fixed-width columns as well as a single variable-width column. As the browser window expands, only one column width expands with it. The layout of the center column shifts, while the two flanking columns stay fixed.

The grid system on SimpleArt.com.au is flexible, so whether the page is viewed on large or small monitors the layout feels consistent. Note in the wider layout below, the columns of the grid widen and the header/navigation area moves to the right.

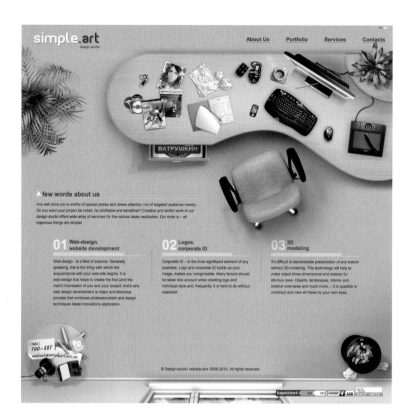

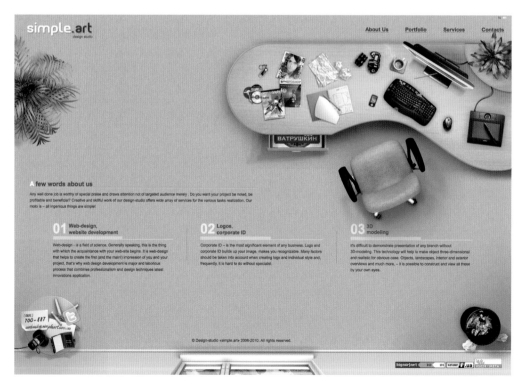

Once the grid system has been established, elements of the design are placed within the grid. Objects can span more than one column width, but each element must have some clear relationship to the grid itself. Any element that relates to the grid in a unique way or breaks the grid system will rank higher on the hierarchy scale.

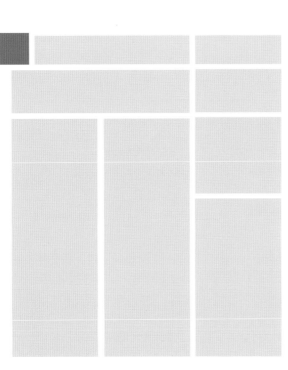

Items in a layout that break the established system stand apart from the rest of the elements within the system. In this example of AIGALosAngelese.org, the AIGA logo does not "sit" on the grid. By shifting outside the grid it's given more visual value than the other elements on the page, as illustrated in this diagram.

The Baseline Grid

Something that print designers have been using for years but is only recently being adopted by Web designers is the use of a baseline grid. A baseline grid is a horizontal grid system that exactly aligns the baselines of all the text on a page, regardless of size or style. Baseline grids create a smooth rhythm in the typography within a design.

Creating a baseline grid in CSS involves a bit of math, since there's no built-in baseline grid attribute. A Web designer starts by choosing a type size for the majority of the text on the page. Then a line height is applied in the CSS, which is essentially the equivalent of leading. To create the appearance of a baseline grid, all other measurements, including the margin spacing, display type size, etc., should be multiples of the line height. This will ensure that all baselines will line up relative to one another.

TheGridSystem.org is a blog about the use of grids in design. An interesting feature of this site is the ability to expose the grid structure as well as the baseline grid.

Below is an example of a baseline grid in use. Note that each typographic element, regardless of size or typeface, sits exactly on the baseline grid.

Above the Fold

Understanding the Principles of Successful Web Site Design

The wizard quickly jinxed the gnomes before they vaporized. All questions asked by five watched experts amaze the judge.

Jaded zombies acted quietly but kept driving their oxen forward. The wizard quickly jinxed the gnomes before they vaporized. All questions asked by five watched experts amaze the judge. Six boys guzzled cheap raw plum vodka quite joyfully. Just keep examining every low bid quoted for zinc etchings. Sixty zippers were quickly picked from the woven jute bag. Few black taxis drive up major roads on quiet hazy nights. Six big devils from Japan quickly forgot how to waltz. Painful zombies quickly watch a jinxed graveyard. Jaded zombies acted quietly but kept driving their oxen forward. The wizard quickly jinxed the gnomes before they vaporized. All questions asked by five watched experts amaze the judge. Six boys guzzled cheap raw plum vodka quite joyfully. Just keep examining every low bid quoted for zinc etchings. Sixty zippers were quickly picked from the woven jute bag. Few black taxis drive up major roads on quiet hazy nights. Six big devils from Japan quickly forgot how to waltz. Painful zombies quickly watch a jinxed graveyard.

Modularity

Modularity can mean a couple of things when it comes to Web design. For a Web designer, modularity means creating reusable or modular design assets that fit within the established grid system and get reused throughout a site. These modules not only create design efficiencies, but they also help with usability by repeating recognizable elements that a user can remember.

This design for CNN.com from the late 2000s employed white modules of content on a gray background. The modules could expand and contract based on the length and priority of content as seen in this three-consecutive-day span following the 2008 U.S. elections.

Modularity can also refer to the necessary design flexibility required in Web design. Some types of Web sites, like news portals, need to accommodate varying lengths and types of content from day to day—even from hour to hour. Therefore, Web design systems for these sites must be flexible to expand and contract as the needs of a site change. This isn't a Web-specific principle; newspapers, magazines, and even corporate identity systems need to have an element of modularity to be effective. What is unique about the Web is the speed with which items in a design need to change (which makes planning ahead an essential part of Web design), the fact that the user can sometimes control the content, and the need for expansion and contraction, making the ultimate outcome unpredictable. Sites that have user-controlled modularity use JavaScript technology to enable users to drag and drop content "blocks" above and below the fold to create their own hierarchy of information.

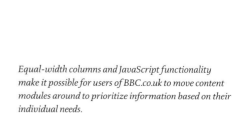

Equal-width columns and JavaScript functionality make it possible for users of BBC.co.uk to move content modules around to prioritize information based on their individual needs.

CHAPTER 4

THE ELEMENTS OF WEB DESIGN

Creating a design system so that dissimilar types of content appear to work together is what graphic designers have been doing for centuries, and Web design is no different. The previous chapter explored various structural and spacial methods of organizing space and creating a structure. Design is about more than simply organizing information, however; it's about making something distinctive and memorable. This chapter explores the aesthetic treatment of the elements within a design that not only help form relationships within a system but create a visual style.

Web Design Style

A design style is an attempt at connecting with a user's sensibilities and a basic need to relate to things. The elements of a design style include color, texture, typography, and imagery use. Additionally, there are means of manipulating these elements including creating a sense of scale, or depth; animation; and variation. The crafting and manipulation of these aesthetic elements of style make a particular design unique, and better yet, memorable.

In all forms of design, a style comes primarily from two areas: the trends of the time—what's fashionable; and the technology that's available to create a piece of design. In graphic design, which dates back to cave paintings and carries on through the carved letterforms on Trajan's column, handwritten manuscripts, Gutenberg's movable type, right on through to photo reproduction and the modern computer age, has always been heavily influenced by the technology available to produce it.

The same is true in Web design. As computer technology, browsing software and the mark up language that makes up a design become more advanced, they influence the design styles and trends. Through it all, however, great design defined by the fundamental understanding of the hierarchical structure that makes up a layout, explored in the previous chapter, combined with the elements of style that give a design its uniqueness.

This page from the Gutenberg Bible, the first Western example of movable type printing, represented state-of-the-art technology when it was produced in the 1450s.

Color

More than any other design element, color has the ability to guide, direct, and persuade a user. In addition to its instructive qualities, color can appeal to a user's emotions by setting a mood or a tone for a piece of design. Colors signify meaning for many people and cultures, making it a powerful tool for designers. The immediacy with which color can be recognized makes it valuable for forming clear relationships.

Color has three main properties: hue, which is commonly known as the color; value, which is the darkness or lightness; and saturation, which is the vibrancy of a color. Because Web design is based on the colors of light (red, blue, and green), the range of colors is greater than with print design, which uses the reflective palette (cyan, magenta, yellow, and black). Although there's a broader color palette, predicting the exact color a user sees is difficult because of variations among monitors and operating systems.

Color is used in Summer.TNVacation.com as a device to emotionally connect with a user. The bright, vibrant colors are intended to excite and engage the user in the summertime activities that Tennessee has to offer.

Relationships of color help users create associations among otherwise unrelated elements within a design.

Color is an excellent way to create relationships within a design. BygoneBureau.com uses colored type to signify various categories; yellow for arts, blue for travel, orange for humor, etc. This use of color helps users quickly scan a page to find information without the need for a lot of reading.

Contrasting color can help a designer guide and direct a user through a layout.

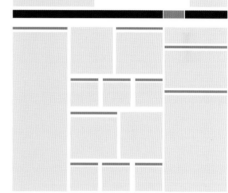

Effectively using color doesn't necessarily mean creating a colorful design. This example, NewYorkMag.com, uses only touches of red among a sea of black and white to lead the user and highlight key information. The schematic (above right) illustrates how color guides the eye down and around the page.

Texture

Adding texture to a Web design gives the user sense of a tactile experience and helps connect him or her to the content of a page. Types of texture can range from smooth, shiny buttons that are common in Web 2.0 design, to rough or grungy treatments, to type imagery or backgrounds. Aside from the stylistic treatments of texture, it's important to remember that on a macro level, every design has a texture, intended or not. Type, images, and illustrations combine to make an overall texture that the user perceives on a subconscious level.

Fall.TWVacation.com has a cubist background texture featuring colors that remind the user of the changing leaves of fall.

Adding texture to a Web design gives the user the sense of a **tactile experience** and helps connect him or her to the content of a page.

The rough metallic texture of VegasUncorked.com gives each page a uniquely identifiable trait in addition to adding depth to the page.

Imagery & Iconography

Studies show that users don't read Web sites, they scan them. For Web designers, the use of images or iconography can mean replacing wordy descriptions with single images, making a layout easier for a user to quickly get information from. A designer's choice of imagery should be deliberate and add either to the branding or the message of the page. All images add to a Web page's weight or file size, so gratuitous use of generic imagery can impede a good user experience.

This page for the iMac on Apple.com integrates type and image in such a way that it looks as if the type is wrapping around the image.

Iconongraphy and imagery enhance the user's experience on TheyMakeApps.com by replacing wordy descriptions with simple and identifiable icons.

The layout for ClutchMagOnline.com relies heavily on photographic thumbnails to make the pages easily scannable. At a glimpse, users can browse the topics of the current issue simply by perusing the photos.

(Opposite) Hand-drawn illustrations combined with photography layered under the content of the page make the side-scrolling site as energetic and dynamic as the music it represents.

Pictured here are three images featuring the iPad from Apple. Each uses scale, but the method of achieving a dramatic sense of scale is slightly different. On the far left, extreme perspective is used to give a sense of depth and make the iPad seem larger than life. In the image on this page, the iPad is the dominant element on the page simply because it's the largest when compared to the other elements. Finally, on the right, the iPads are breaking out of the defined border, making them feel too large to be contained within the space.

Scale

Contrast of size or scale is one way designers can add a sense of drama to a design. Having a dominant element is critical to creating a clear sequence or hierarchy of elements within a design. Scale is a relative design element, so in order to achieve a dynamic feeling of scale, small elements must be included in the layout for comparison's sake. Large design elements that break out of borders or even bleed off the page also heighten the sense of scale.

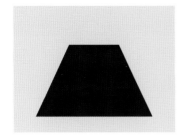
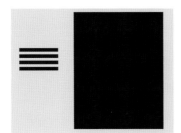
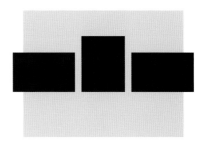

In this example from FamousCookies.com, the larger-than-life cookies and typography combine with the smaller elements on the page to create a dramatic sense of scale and appetite appeal.

In these examples, JasonSantaMaria.com (top) and OldGuard.co.uk, a dominant design element is used as a focal point to the page. This use of scale pulls the user in, inviting him or her to explore the other elements on the page.

Depth & Dimension

There are many ways to create the illusion of depth in a Web design. From overlapping design elements, to adding gradient color and shadows, to creating three-dimensional elements, adding depth to a Web page can help add visual interest and draw a user into a design. Applying depth and dimension to a page gives it an element of realism, and, like texture, gives the user a more tactile experience.

This Web page for developer Oliver James Gosling (goslingo.com) gives new meaning to the phrase "above the fold." The subtle gradations of gray and cast shadowing give the appearance of an unfolded brochure.

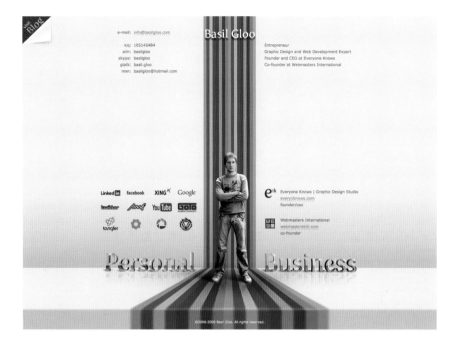

The sites pictured here use color and perspective to create a dynamic and colorful sense of depth. The site above, BasilGloo.com, uses photography and three-dimensional type to create a realistic environment. The site to the left, for Joshua Keckley, uses shadowing and texture to achieve a similar, yet less realistic, effect. Both sites use a focal point to draw the user into the layout.

From three-dimensional type and objects in perspective, to layered elements and subtle gradations of color and shadowing, Syfy.com appears to be completely designed around the concept of depth and dimension. Almost every element of the design seems to lift off the screen. The main feature area is a shelf where elements stand, casting a shadow onto the other pieces of information.

From overlapping design elements and adding gradient color and shadows to creating three-dimensional elements, adding depth to a Web page can help add **visual interest** and draw a user into a design.

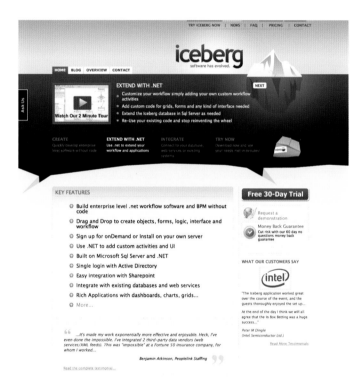

This site for Iceberg Software features an illustration of an iceberg drawn in perspective and used to draw the user into the page, and, more specifically, the focal point which is the company logo. This layout achieves a sense of depth not only through perspective but through color value. The darker colors appear closer and the fainter tones recede into the background.

Animation

Animation is a tool used by digital designers to layer information, create a sequence of information, or simply surprise and delight the user. Animation can be the focal point of a design—like a slideshow or video in the main feature area—but animation can also be simple and subtle, like small amounts of movement when a user mouses over a button. Too much repetitive animation, especially on pages with a lot of content, can become distracting to a user. Web design best practices dictate that the designer should always give the user the ability to pause a large animation, or, if an animation is looping, to cycle for no more than three cycles.

ShoeGuru.com uses a very simple sliding slideshow animation for the feature area of the home page. The twist comes from the sense of space that's established with the horizon line and the shadowing under the images.

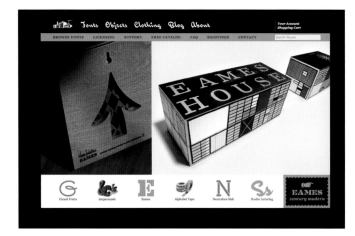

The Web site for House Industries (HouseInd.com) has two vertical slideshows on the home page set with slightly different timing. The variation in timing creates multiple side-by-side images that mix and match randomly.

Both ShoeGuru.com (left) and HouseInd.com (right) utilize a common slideshow convention, but both use them in unique ways that appear fresh and original.

The large central slideshow on TMagazine. com, the Web site for the New York Times Magazine, not only adds visual interest to the page, but the scale of the imagery gives the site a magazine feel.

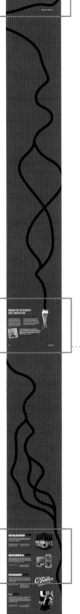

BountyBev.com takes users on a journey down a road by using animation for the main site navigation. When a user clicks "NEXT," the single-page Web site scrolls down, stopping at the next area.

Author's note: It's entirely unclear to me why a road and a driving metaphor are appropriate for a beer company, but the value of the design made it hard to resist including in the book. Enjoy responsibly.

Variability

The speed at which a Web designer can apply changes, combined with the need to continually refresh the look of a site, gives Web designers the ability to vary elements of a design based on things like sections of the site or specific events—or randomly. What was once considered unthinkable—altering a corporate logo, for example—can now be a playful way to add relevance to a Web site. The best way to keep a site fresh is by updating the content. But if that's not possible, design variations can give the user the impression that a site is fresh and current.

The logo on Typophile.com reflects the wide variety of typography represented on their site.

The header of the Web site for the American Institute
of Graphic Arts features images of design work from
their archive. The images randomly appear, giving the
site a fresh look each time a user visits the page.

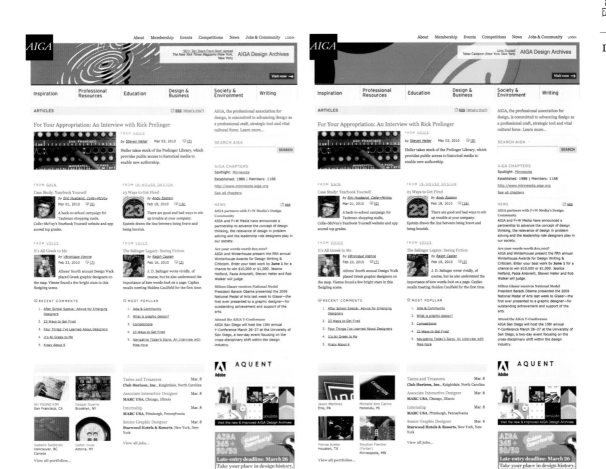

What was once considered to be **unthinkable** can now be a playful way to add relevance and variety.

These images from Google.com show the playfulness with which their designers treat the Google branding, from the anniversary of the moon landing to Dr. Seuss' birthday.

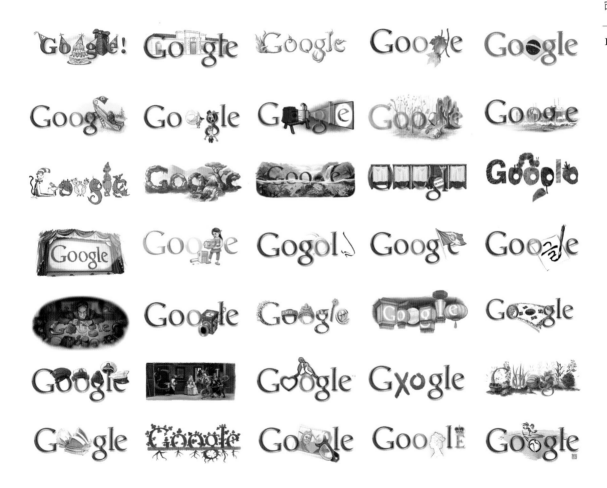

*The Web site for the Maryland Institute College of Art, MICA.edu, offers the
ability to select from four student project thumbnail images along the top of the
page. Each selection completely alters not only the images but the color scheme
of the page. The color palette is derived from each piece of student work. In this
case, the variability is user controlled and conceptually it highlights the main
constituents of the school: the students.*

In this case, the variability is controlled by the user, and conceptually it highlights the main constituents of the school: **the students.**

CHAPTER 5

WEB TYPOGRAPHY

"Typography is the one area in graphic design where there are truly rights and wrongs; there are better-thans and there are randoms.**"**

Alexander W. White
Chairman Emeritus, The Type Directors Club

S1
Design &
Typography

S2
Planning
& Usability

S3
Business
Effectiveness

Why Type Matters

Typography, of all elements of design, can have the greatest effect on the success or failure of a piece of communication. This is because type carries the message, and the craftsmanship of the typography can either enhance or take away from the message. Many designers share a passion for the art of typography and can spend hours kerning letters, adjusting the rag on a column of type, or hanging punctuation. With Web design, however, this level of finite control is difficult, or in some cases not possible at all. But before examining the specific nuances of Web type, it's important to understand a few universal principals of typography.

It has been said that great typography is invisible, but that's only half the story—typography can also be beautifully expressive and attention grabbing. In either case, type must carry a message to the user. The two opposing characteristics, which combine to attract a user and convey a message, are called readability and legibility. Both are essential for effective communication.

Readability refers to how well type can attract a reader. Typographic posters, book covers, packaging, logos, and magazine features, for example, must have a readable quality to them to in order to get the attention of a reader—a quality that makes a person stop and want to read. Readability can come from size, font usage, composition, color usage, abstraction, or anything that helps type—or, more specifically, the message—stand apart. Effectively readable type expresses meaning through form beyond the content of the words it displays. The FedEx logo is an example of this idea. The bold, geometric shapes of the letterforms imply stability or reliability, while the negative-space arrow between the capital *E* and lowercase *x* implies forward moving and speed—all this with only the use of five letters and two colors.

The FedEx logo, pictured here and designed by Landor Associates, depicts both stability and forward moving with simple yet very readable type.

WebMD.com offers users the ability to change the size of type within an article. This allows the user to control the optimal legibility based on his or her preferences—a concept not possible with conventional print communications. The images below show small, medium, and large type sizes.

Legibility, on the other hand, references the ease with which a reader can gather a message, especially when it comes to long stretches of copy. The recognizability of individual characters in a font as well as type size, leading, letter spacing, line length—even color and backgrounds—play a role in how effectively legible type appears. Truly legible type makes it possible for the reader to only perceive content and not be distracted by formatting or decoration.

These two aspects of type play a big part in effective Web typography; however, the level of control a designer has and the methods he or she uses to achieve them can be very different. Readable or expressive typography can be important on the home page to grab the user's attention, define a unique brand characteristic, or alert the reader to a site feature or special offer. Legible type is essential for article or blog text, and can make the difference in the success of a site that invites users to return to read long articles or posts.

While there are limitations to the control a designer has over typographic details on the Web, there are also methods, unique to Web design, of turning over control to the user so he or she may create personalized settings for legibility. Many sites give users the ability to change the size of text, and some sites even give users the option of choosing their own fonts. This idea of user control, even over typographic decisions, is explored further in Chapter 6, "Interactivity and Customization," and is the core of what effective Web design is all about—balancing brand and design aesthetics with the needs and desires of the user.

Measuring Type

Type and typographic properties such as spacing are commonly measured in em units. An em is a square unit that represents the distance between baselines when type is set without line spacing or leading. An em square is equal to the size of the type; for example, an em space for 12 pixel/point type is a 12-pixel square.

While an em is equal to the type size, the individual characters don't necessarily fit within an em square—they can be larger or smaller. As seen in the diagram below, a Dispatch M fits within a single em unit of 110 points, however the Burgues Script M at the same size is not confined to the em unit.

In Web design—more specifically, CSS styling—type can be defined using em units. Ems are used for relative sizing and for type they're used in the font-size attribute.

Most browsers default to 16-pixel type as a general rule. So if a designer specs type at 75 percent, the size of the type will be 12 pixels. The default can also be altered globally by styling the <body> tag. If in the body tag the font size is set to 62.5 percent, then the default for all type on a site is 10 pixels (16 x .625 = 10). Therefore, the math for defining other sizes become easier: for 15 pixel type the font-size would be set to 1.5 em; 24-pixel type would be 2.4 em, etc.

110-pt. Dispatch

110-pt. Burgues Script

The optimal choice for displaying type depends mostly on the **needs the client** and the **capabilities of the target user.**

Types of Web Type

When it comes to rendering type on the Web, a designer has three primary options:

- Images of type
- Web-safe fonts
- Font replacement and embedding

These options represent a spectrum of control, with designer control at one end and user control at the other. The optimal choice depends mostly on the needs a client has for the site, and the capabilities and needs of the target user. The ultimate solution for displaying type usually involves a carefully considered combination of all three options.

Designer Control   User Control

Images of type
(chirp.twitter.com)

Font replacement
(typekit.com)

Type and image
combination
(branding.sva.edu)

Web-safe type
(seedconference.com)

This image of MidtSommerJazz.no shows all three methods of displaying type on the Web—images, Web safe fonts, and embedded fonts.

Using images to display type is a static method of rendering type—the type is rendered once by the designer or producer, and that image is distributed throughout the Web to be viewed by the user. Using Web-safe fonts is a means of displaying content as live text, which is rendered by the user's browser. Live text generally offers less control to the designer but more control to the user with which to manipulate aesthetics and/or search the content. Various means of embedded fonts—which give a designer the ability to select a wide range of typefaces while still rendering live text— have recently emerged.), Since this represents the latest advance in Web technology, some browsers are yet to support these methods of embedding fonts and therefore some users cannot see them.

Why is this choice so significant? The reason selecting a method with which to display type is so critical to Web design is due to the fact that type delivers content and content drives the success of most Web sites. Content is what users search for. Content is what search engines index and catalog, and search engines can only pull content from live text—images of type are not indexable by search engines. Content, however, must be dressed with some form of style or branding in order to be truly effective for the Web site's owner. Purely displaying content without some sort of visual expressiveness or uniqueness decreases its memorability and therefore decreases its value to the client. The following pages explore examples of each method of displaying type, and details the benefits and drawbacks for each.

The home page of chirp.twitter.com is almost completely made up of imagery. Only the navigation and a newsletter signup are Web safe. This approach is effective in part because the site didn't need to rely on search engines for traffic. Instead, users were alerted to the site using viral methods—word-of-mouth campaigns that spread through social networking.

Image Type

Images of type offer a Web designer the most control over the typography on a Web page. A designer can freely choose a font from his or her library, adjust the kerning, add filters and effects, etc.—all the things that traditional print designers are used to doing with type. Images of type enable a designer to match exactly branding requirements for a client, or just to simply express a concept exactly as the designer (or client) envisions.

Interior pages of the Chirp Conference mini-site use an effective combination of illustrative type and Web-safe fonts.

There are a couple of significant drawbacks with this method of displaying type, however. All-image Web sites, where the type is rendered as a jpg, png, or gif image, are extremely limited in their ability to be indexed by search engines, and thus limited in their ability to be found by users. While it's possible to include searchable content within the alt tags—a tag within the image tag that allows the Webmaster to input text describing an image, used mainly for handicapped accessibility—this text does not have a high value with search engines because it can too easily be manipulated to deceive the user.

CreatureBox.com is the portfolio Web site for illustrators Dave Guertin and Greg Baldwin. Their expressive, illustrative style comes through in this Web site that uses a dynamic mix of hand-drawn elements and Web typography.

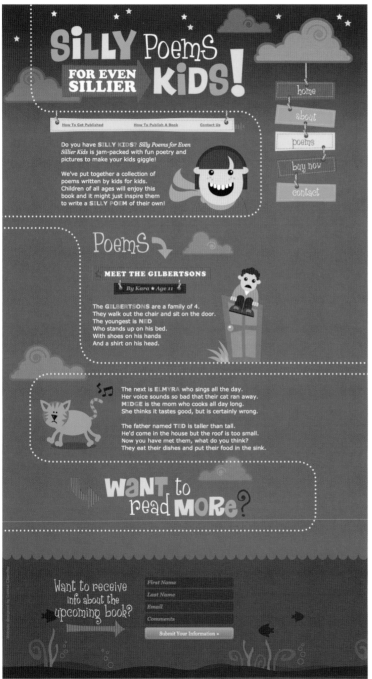

Silly Poems for Even Sillier Kids! uses a variety of fonts displayed as images to create a fun and childlike image on this Web site. While the main content is set in Web-safe Verdana with touches of Georgia, the display type, which anchors the page along with the illustrations, are images.

Images of type enable a designer to exactly **match branding requirements** for a client, or **express a concept** precisely as the designer (or client) envisions.

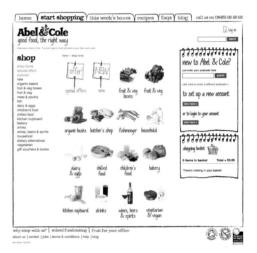

To create a handmade or organic feel to the design, the designers of AbelandCole.co.uk used images of hand-lettered type.

BearSkinRug.co.uk is a Web site featuring the work of designer and illustrator Kevin Cornell. The hand-drawn lettering throughout the site reflects the content and style of the artist. What makes this site stand out is not only the hand-drawn lettering, but the clear sense of hierarchy and space.

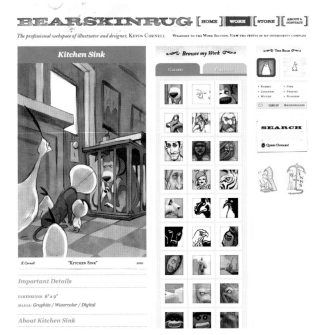

The best approach for using images as type on a Web site is to limit the use to particular areas of display type where the images can have the most visual impact. Commonly, designers choose to use images of type for the main navigation of the site; however, this is particularly damaging as search engines place a high value on linked content. If the main links are images, the links' value cannot be captured by search engines. The bottom line is that images of type are a great way to add personality or brand recognition to a Web site, but should be used extremely sparingly in order to maintain the searchability of a site.

The identity for the Branding graduate program at the School of Visual Arts is distinctive, creative, and could not be replicated using only Web-safe type. The solution here is to integrate enough of the custom lettering to maintain the recognizability of the brand with Web-safe type for legibility and searchability.

Web-Safe Type

In historical terms, a font is a complete set of characters that makes up a single size, style, and weight of a typeface. The term typeface refers to the unique styling applied to a set of glyphs, including an alphabet of letters and ligatures, numerals, and punctuation marks. Due largely to their use in relation to computers, the two terms have evolved to be interchangeable. The term *font* no longer refers to a single size or style, and can even refer to the digital file used by the computer to display typefaces.

There are literally thousands of fonts available to designers. However, choosing a font to display live text on a Web site usually means choosing a font that exists on the user's computer. These fonts are called *Web-safe fonts*. While Web-safe fonts vary slightly in appearance from Mac to PC—and their display varies from browser to browser—the general appearance is consistent enough that a designer can reasonably predict the look of the finished design when viewed by the user.

Windows	Mac
Arial	Arial, Helvetica
Arial Black	Arial Black, Gadget
Comic Sans MS	Comic Sans MS
Courier New	Courier New, Courier
Georgia	Georgia
Impact	Impact, Charcoal
Lucida Console	Monaco
Lucida Sans Unicode	Lucida Grande
Palatino Linotype	Palatino
Book Antiqua	Georgia
Tahoma	Tahoma
Times New Roman	Times
Trebuchet MS	Trebuchet MS
Verdana	Verdana
Symbol	Symbol
Webdings	Webdings
Wingdings	Zapf Dingbats
MS Sans Serif	Geneva
MS Serif	Georgia

Being able to do **more with less** is an essential skill for a Web designer.

This all-type solution for the Seed Conference announcement showcases many of the possibilities of CSS type styling. Varying type sizes, colors, and alignments create a clear hierarchy within a unified piece of design.

Designers define a Web-safe font using what is called a *font stack*. Font stacks are prioritized lists of fonts, defined in the CSS font-family attribute, that the browser will cycle through until it finds a font that is installed on the user's system. Font stacks list fonts in order of the designer's preference: preferred, alternate, common, generic. Common font stacks include:

Verdana, Arial, Helvetica, sans-serif

Tahoma, Geneva, Arial, sans-serif

Georgia, Times New Roman, Times, serif

Palatino Linotype, Book Antiqua, Palatino, serif

Courier New, Courier, monospace

Lucida Console, Monaco, Courier, monospace

The limitations and unpredictability of font stacks present a challenge to Web designers. Limitations also lead to creative solutions. Doing more with less is an essential skill for a Web designer. The sites pictured here represent a wide visual language using only Web-safe typography.

Jason Santa Maria is considered to be one of Web design's most creative talents. Pictured here are two pages from his site, JasonSantaMaria.com, where he displays his mastery over type, Web type, and imagery integration.

Daytum.com uses large, bold, Web-safe type to create a distinctive look for the site. This creates a clear hierarchy of information, making the pages easily scannable by the user.

ALListApart.com, a blog for Web designers and developers, exploits the full potential of Web-safe typography with an elegant mix of fonts and styles that blend together to create a cohesive design with a clear informational hierarchy.

Portico
front page

Home
sweet home

Archive
and search

Contact
and email

Subscribe
via rss

1 OPTIMIZATION VS. HARDWARE PROCUREMENT
How buying hardware is often the cheapest way to solve computational complexity.

2 NEW FEATURES OF C# 4.0 *by Mads Torgersen*
True dynamic typing and type safe co- & contra-variance

3 N-CORE PERFORMANCE TO PLATEAU *by R Murphy*
Could off-die memory latency one day force fundamental changes to architectures?

· Promo ·   · Preface ·

hire
ME

TYPESETTING
GRAPHIC / .NET WIN & WEB
DESIGN / DEVELOPMENT

OH, HELLO. HERE LIE A
COLLECTION OF ARTICLES,
NARRATIVES AND
PONDERINGS OF COMPUTERY
THINGS; FINELY BLENDED
WITH MY PORTFOLIO
BESTOWING WORKS AND
EXPERIMENTS IN U.I. DESIGN,
INFOGRAPHICS, AND
SOFTWARE DEVELOPMENT.
BON APPÉTIT.

· Calendar ·

<< MAY 2010 >>
MO	TU	WE	TH	FR	SA	SU
					1	2
3	4	5	6	7	8	9
10	11	12	13	14	15	16
17	18	19	20	21	22	23
24	25	26	27	28	29	30
31						

· Categories ·

	POSTS	RSS
CYNOSURA	0	RSS
GENERAL	0	RSS
GRAPHIC DESIGN	4	RSS
PROGRAMMING	5	RSS
WWW TECH	2	RSS

Raymond S. Glover
Cynosura

THE ARCHIVES

10 ENTRIES SPANNING 1 YEAR, 2 MONTHS, 1 WEEK,
1 DAY AND 11 HOURS

Enter search term

SEARCH

☐ INCLUDE COMMENTS IN SEARCH

CATEGORY	RSS
1. Cynosura	subscribe
2. General	subscribe
3. Graphic Design	subscribe
4. Programming	subscribe
5. WWW Tech	subscribe

1. Cynosura

DATE	TITLE	COMMENTS	RATING
	Total	0	NONE

2. General

DATE	TITLE	COMMENTS	RATING
	Total	0	NONE

3. Graphic Design

DATE	TITLE	COMMENTS	RATING
2009-09-19	RENDERING LONDON	7	4
2009-03-01	PIXELS IN VECTORS	23	4.5
2009-01-31	GROWTH RATES	10	5
2008-12-29	DICTIONARY UI MOCKUPS	3	4.6
	Total	43	4.5

4. Programming

DATE	TITLE	COMMENTS	RATING
2010-03-06	JSON PRETTY PRINTER	0	NONE
2009-03-02	SOCKETS AND C#	15	4
2009-01-27	THE TIMESPAN ARTICULATOR	5	5
2008-12-28	THE COWON S9; REVERSE ENGINEERED	14	4.5
2008-12-26	A LINE MAPPING STREAMREADER	3	NONE
	Total	37	4.5

5. WWW Tech

DATE	TITLE	COMMENTS	RATING
2009-09-19	RENDERING LONDON	7	4
2008-12-30	THE SEMANTIC WEB	17	4.8
	Total	24	4.4

Overview

10 posts by 2 author(s)
97 comments by 86 reader(s)
39 raters averaging 4.6

Weblog.Cynosura.eu seemlessly mixes images of type with Web-safe type—with the majority shown here being Web safe. The centered layout and delicate line work give the site a classic beauty.

Portico
front page

Home
sweet home

Archive
and search

Contact
and email

Subscribe
via rss

LAT

1 OPTIMIZATION VS. HARDWARE PROCUREMENT
How buying hardware is often the cheapest way to solve computational complexity.

2 NEW FEATURES OF C# 4.0 *by Mads Torgersen*
True dynamic typing and type safe co- & contra-variance

3 N-CORE PERFORMANCE TO PLATEAU *by R Murphy*
Could off-die memory latency one day force fundamental changes to architectures?

· Promo ·   · Preface ·

hire
ME

TYPESETTING
GRAPHIC / .NET WIN & WEB
DESIGN / DEVELOPMENT

OH, HELLO. HERE LIE A
COLLECTION OF ARTICLES,
NARRATIVES AND
PONDERINGS OF COMPUTERY
THINGS; FINELY BLENDED
WITH MY PORTFOLIO
BESTOWING WORKS AND
EXPERIMENTS IN U.I. DESIGN,
INFOGRAPHICS, AND
SOFTWARE DEVELOPMENT.
BON APPÉTIT.

· Calendar ·   · Categories ·

JSON

Does what is says on t
year ago after a failed
light and simple JS n

Font Replacement & Embedding

Font replacement is emerging as a way to give designers the most typographic flexibility with their design, while still being able to take advantage of the searchability of live text. There are three primary methods of embedding or replacing fonts within a Web layout: Flash- and image-based replacement methods like sIFR; the @font-face css command; or JavaScript replacement like Cufón or TypeKit.

Early forms of font replacement included a Flash-based system called sIFR. sIFR replaces a specific tag, like an <H1> tag for example, with a swf file containing rendering information for a specific font. This method worked but it requires the end user to have the Flash plugin installed and there was some lag between when the page loaded and when the replacement font appeared.

MICA.edu uses an elegant combination of sIFR and Web-safe fonts to create a well-organized and typographically rich layout.

Fonts represent **valuable intellectual property** and @font-face leaves some question as to the end user's ability to reuse the font without paying for it.

Although the @font-face command existed in CSS2 and dates back to 1998, it wasn't supported by most browsers. With the release of CSS3, more browsers have included the @font-face functionality. The @font-face CSS command is a two-step process that involves first defining a path to a font on the server. This is done in a similar way to defining a background image, for example, by using the src or source call in CSS. Once the path to the font has been identified, it's simply a matter of calling the font when defining other tags.

```
@font-face {
      font-family: "Dispatch";
      src: url(http://www.WebSite.com/fonts/dispatch.ttf);
      format("truetype");
}

h1 { font-family: "Dispatch", sans-serif }
```

Above is sample CSS code showing how @font-face is implemented by first defining the path to a font, then calling that font in a font stack for a particular tag.

The @font-face command seems like the perfect solution to a nagging problem for Web designers. However, this method of uploading a font on a server and allowing users to access it for the purposes of viewing a single Web site is causing some concern among those who design and license typefaces. Fonts represent valuable intellectual property and this method leaves some question as to the end users' ability to reuse the font without paying for it. Very few fonts allow linking in CSS in their copyright agreement, so while the technology is ready, the legal implications of linking fonts is far from resolved.

Subscription-based services, such as Typekit. com, are emerging to deal with the issue of font licensing while still giving Web designers the ability to legally implement the @font-face functionality. Typekit is a service that charges a yearly fee which gives designers access to a library of Web-licensed fonts. Designers chose the font or fonts from this library that they would like displayed in their Web design and are given a line of JavaScript code. Since the path to the fonts is not being displayed in the CSS, the fonts are protected from illegal downloading.

Typekit.com offers subscription-based access to fonts for Web sites, including fonts from TypeTogether's font foundry, also seen here.

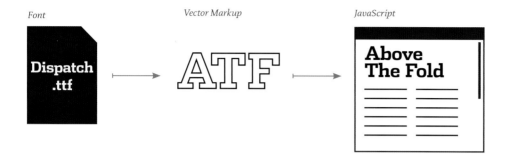

Font   Vector Markup   JavaScript

Above is a diagram showing how Cufón works by uploading a font to a server, converted to VML (Vector Markup Language), and called to a Web page using JavaScript.

Another JavaScript-based method of font replacement is called Cufón. Cufón works by converting font informations into VML (Vector Markup Language), which is rendered and displayed on the users's computer. This proprietary JavaScript function prevents the end user from ever downloading the font, avoiding issues of redistribution. Cufón is the fastest JavaScript solution yet, since the VML is roughly 75 percent of the original file size of the font. It's also supported by most of the latest browser versions. Perhaps most importantly, Cufón generates searchable, selectable type while displaying any font in a designer's library.

Bridgeport.edu/SASD uses Cufón for various headlines, diagrammatic copy, and the navigation.

Although Cufón is the most widely used font replacement method, it has its limitations. Copyright issues still apply. Designers must be sure that the fonts they upload to the Cufón server can be used for Web display.

Copyright issues aside, not all fonts are effective for on-screen legibility. Web-safe fonts were designed specifically to be viewed in backlit situations with larger x-heights, open counters, and wider letter spacing. These factors must be considered when choosing alternatives to Web safe fonts. Much like the "desktop publishing" explosion of the late 1980s, the Web font revolution has the potential to pollute the landscape of Web design as much as beautify it.

Action starts with Attention.

562,522,871 SECONDS
of attention delivered by VideoEgg to help eliminate AIDS in Africa

Help eliminate AIDS in Africa. Join (RED) and VideoEgg in support of The Lazarus Effect film. Learn more about (RED).

+ Share this page

Red.VideoEgg.com uses the @font-face CSS command to display several non-Web-safe fonts in this layout, including Trade Gothic and URW Typewriter.

We Deliver Attention

(RED) challenged us to raise awareness for The Lazarus Effect film that premieres on May 24 on HBO, YouTube and Channel 4 (UK). Here are the real-time results from across the **VideoEgg Engagement Network.**

The Campaign

Average time per user session: **24.2 seconds**

Impressions delivered	10,139,915
Discrete engagements	134,794
Total video views	148,799
Secondary actions taken	4,280

> Where does this data come from?

Our Creative Strategy

VideoEgg started with the (RED) assets and put this campaign together across the web and mobile.

Online campaign:

(RED)

Roll over to replay

Mobile campaign:

+

> Download 'Scrambled' app and check it out!

DOC · We are also running AdFrames DOC takeover ads on key sites across the VideoEgg network. **Click to check out the DOC ad.**

Our Media Strategy

Objective: Drive awareness, content consumption, social network engagement
Target: Broad reach to P13+ IN US, UK and .CA

☐ 25% Doc
☐ 10% Mobile
☐ 65% Display

Launch   Heavy-Up   Sustain

May 18   Premiere Day - May 24   June 30

You Take Action

We're asking everyone to get involved to help raise awareness about The Lazarus Effect film which shows the power of 2 life-saving pills that cost around 40¢/day. Watch, share, tweet, grab, post, like, promote.

Grab and Share: 40¢ = 2 life-saving pills

40¢ = 2 life-saving pills | 20p = 2 life-saving pills | Lazarus Effect Trailer

▶ 🔊 0:00 / 1:01

Embed **40¢ = 2 life-saving pills** on your site:
`<object style="height: 344px; width: 425px>`

👍 Like ✉

137,614
YouTube views

The Lazarus Effect premieres Monday May 24th
HBO and YouTube 9:30pm ET | Channel 4 UK 11pm GMT

Tweet: Get Involved & Help Eliminate AIDS

I SHA(RED) #lazaruseffect. Watch Bono, Don Cheadle & more show the power of 40 cents from @joinred. http://bit.ly/cMQ8qq

Tweet your thoughts here.   TWEET

> Follow (RED)

1,029,307
(RED) followers

VIDEOEGG IS PROUD TO BE A (RED) PROMOTIONAL PARTNER

VideoEgg.com uses Cufón to display much of the typography on the site.

The headlines on BrooklynFare.com, designed by Mucca Design, are rendered using Cufón, while larger areas of body copy and lists rely on Web-safe fonts.

Brooklyn Fare

The Market   The Kitchen   The Café   Catering   Rewards   Specials   About Us

Prepared Foods   Sushi   Produce   Cheese   Meat   Seafood   Beer   Bakery   Grocery   Delivery

For simple foods with restaurant-caliber flavors look no farther than the Brooklyn Fare kitchen.

That's where you'll find César Ramirez and his staff whipping up surprising fare at surprisingly low prices. They turn the fresh ingredients from our market into extraordinary meals. It's the sort of food that makes your dinner table, couch or cubicle feel like the best seat in Brooklyn.

Stop in for a taste, or check out our weekly menu below.

Gourmet Salads
(small 8 oz. - large 16 oz.)

	S	L
Roasted & Marinated Beets toasted walnuts, roquefort cheese	4	7
Toasted Almond Noodle julienne of vegetables, thai basil, cilantro, mango, scallions, sesame vinaigrette	4	7
Cucumber greek yogurt, crème fraiche, fresh dill	4	7
Albacore Tuna homemade mayo, lemon, caper dressing	4	8
Mediterranean olives, feta, tuna, oregano vinaigrette	5	10
Seafood Salad pickled fennel, oven-roasted tomatoes, sicilian oregano vinaigrette	5	10
Tricolore Italian endive, arugula, radicchio, balsamic vinaigrette	4	7
Grilled Chicken Pasta Salad broccoli rabe, toasted garlic dressing (available without chicken)	3	6
French Green Beans crunchy turkish pistachio, shallots, pistachio oil	4	8
Sautéed Broccoli Rabe garlic oil, pepperoncini	4	8
Wilted Baby Spinach freshly grated nutmeg, garlic, shaved grana padano	3	6
Chicken Salad carrots, celery	3	6
Globe Artichoke shaved pecorino, lemon, truffle & black pepper dressing	8	15
Caeser romaine hearts, croutons, shaved parmesan	3	6
Mixed Seasonal asparagus, peas, lemon herb dressing	4	7
Grilled Vegetable seasonal vegetables, creamy balsamic dressing	4	8
Grill Baby Zucchini with fresh mint, tarragon and parsley	4	7
Field Greens naval oranges, mixed nuts, orange dressing	4	8
Oven-Dried Pesto bow-tie pasta, grana padano	4	8
Red Potato Bliss Salad	3	6
Arugula, Pear & Fennel	4	8

Soups

	S	L
Chicken 8 pasta chicken noodle w/ diced vegetables	3	5
Spring Pea	3	5
Seafood Bouillabaisse w/ saffron, market fish	3	5
Lentil & Vegetable w/ vegetable stock, carrot, celery, onions	3	5
Dried Fava Bean vegetarian	3	5
Creamy Corn organic corn chowder	3	5

Main Courses
(small 8 oz. - large 16 oz.)

	S	L
Miso Marinated Atlantic Salmon	5	10
Organic Chicken Breast	4	8
Buttermilk and Breaded Chicken	3	7
Orecchetti & Cheese	3	7
Bolognese Lasagna	6	12
Whole Roasted Organic Chicken with sweet Hungarian paprika	5	8
Eggplant & Mozzarella Lasagna	6	12
Chicken Meat Balls w/ fresh tomato sauce, oregano	3	7
Boneless Short Ribs braised in red wine	8	17

Artisan Sandwiches

Glazed Portobello fresh mozzarella, arugula pesto	8
Lemon Chicken goat cheese, oven-dried tomatoes, walnuts, on a brioche	8
Tuna Salad lettuce, tomatoes, cucumber, on a croissant	7
Grilled Eggplant capers, balsamic, tuna tonnato sauce	8
Grilled Zucchini goat cheese, tomatoes, peppers, lettuce, olive pâté	7
Tomato, Mozzarella basil dressing, on a toasted brioche	8
Stilton sliced pear, fresh arugula	8
Chicken Salad avocado spread, lettuce, bacon	8
Serrano Ham manchego, watercress	8
Grass-Fed Beef white cheddar, glazed sweet onions, horseradish dressing	7
French Brie granny smith apple, celery root rémoulade	7
Cracked Pepper Turkey lettuce, tomatoes, dijon mustard	7
Fish & Chips fried cod, chips, tartar sauce	8
Smoked Ham gruyère, lettuce, honey mustard dressing	7
Speck blue cheese, mission fig spread	8
Smoked Salmon red onion, anchovy or chive yogurt dressing	8

Prices are subject to change without notice.

Because of its speed and light file sizes, not only are the headlines of FestivalBoreal.com rendered using Cufón, longer areas of copy are as well.

Display type on Wineshop.Hunters.co.nz
is replaced using Cufón.

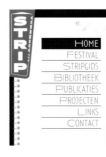

Stripturnhout.be uses Cufón for the left-hand navigation.

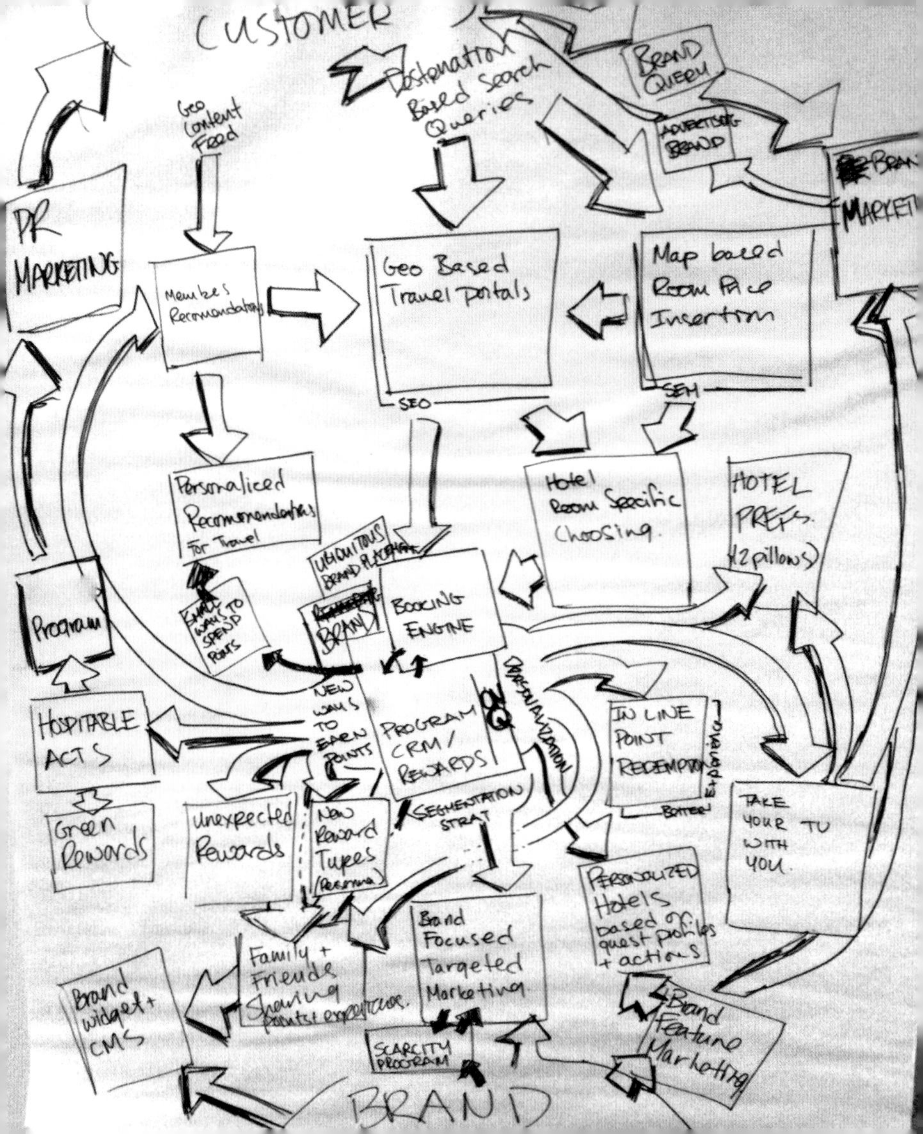

CUSTOMER

Geo Content Feed

Destination Based Search Queries

BRAND QUERY

ADVERTISING BRAND

BRAND MARKETING

PR MARKETING

Member Recommendations

Geo Based Travel Portals

Map based Room Price Insertion

SEO

SEH

Personalized Recommendations for Travel

Hotel Room Specific Choosing

HOTEL PREFS. (2 pillows)

UBIQUITOUS BRAND PLACEMENT

EASY WAY TO SPEND POINTS

BRAND

Booking Engine

Program

NEW WAYS TO EARN POINTS

PROGRAM CRM/ REWARDS

PERSONALIZATION

IN LINE POINT REDEMPTION

BOTTER

Experience

HOSPITABLE ACTS

SEGMENTATION STRAT

TAKE YOUR TV WITH YOU.

Green Rewards

Unexpected Rewards

New Reward Types (Rooms)

PERSONALIZED Hotels based on guest profiles + actions

Brand widget + CMS

Family + Friends Sharing points experiences

Brand Focused Targeted Marketing

SCARCITY PROGRAM

Brand Feature Marketing

BRAND

Section II

PLANNING
& USABILITY

Site Planning

Elements of Usability

CHAPTER 6

SITE PLANNING

User-focused design, or design that puts the user ahead of fancy design treatments or gratuitous use of technology, must start with a plan. The objective of this plan is to align the client's business goals with the needs and desires of the target user group. A plan can also help map out a "big picture" view of the project, giving all members of the team perspective, clarity, and a common goal. Lastly, an effective plan helps remove subjectivity from the creative process and gives a framework for decision-making.

S1
Design &
Typography

S2
Planning
& Usability

S3
Business
Value

Project Planning

Creating a Web site project plan is a multi-part, multi-disciplinary
process. The phases of this process can include research and discovery;
content inventory; site mapping; wireframing; usability mapping;
prototyping; and design concepting, all of which are discussed in
this chapter. Depending on the size of the project, this phase can
take a week to several months to establish the documents needed to
effectively move forward with the design phase.

There are many benefits to developing an effective site plan.
The client should reap long-term benefits from a reduction in the
development cost normally associated with inflexible or flawed
systems, to decreased training costs. These benefits help clients
make the most of their Web site and achieve the highest return on
their investment (ROI).

Plans also help the design team define the parameters of a project for
estimating purposes. Once a plan is in place, the designer or project
team should have a clear picture of the scope of work (SOW) for the
project. The team can then estimate and assign time to each task or
phase of the project. If along the way the client has revisions or changes
direction, the designer or project team can refer back to the approved
plan and determine whether the project needs to be re-estimated or if
the alterations are within the original scope of work.

Ultimately, however, site planning should be about the user. The goal
of a well-conceived site plan is to increase a user's satisfaction with
a site by organizing information and optimizing the critical tasks on
the site. The measure of the ease of use for a site is called *usability*
and is discussed in the next chapter. What follows are the basic steps
involved in the Web site planning stage.

Research & Discovery

The process of developing a plan usually starts with research into the client's goals for the site and an analysis of the landscape in which a site will exist. A briefing meeting is an interview with the client to better understand the purpose behind the project. This can be conducted by a designer or an account executive (also called a client manager), whose job is to manage the client relationship. A SWOT (strengths, weaknesses, opportunities, and threats) analysis can be very helpful in pinpointing the internal and external factors that will influence the project. A SWOT analysis categorizes the internal and external, positive and negative factors that can influence the effectiveness of a site.

To gain a deeper understanding of the landscape, it's often necessary to conduct a competitive analysis and customer interviews. A competitive analysis results in noting what the competition does well as well as where they fall short. This can help identify gaps in the market that the client can take advantage of. Customer interviews are helpful for identifying the current perception of the client organization or the general feeling of the current market.

To the right is an example of a SWOT analysis. The process of developing a SWOT chart can help uncover key pieces of information that help shape the usability and concept of a Web site. Strengths and weaknesses are internal factors, while opportunities and threats are external factors that a client has little control over.

A **SWOT analysis** categorizes the internal
and external, positive and negative factors
that can influence the effectiveness of a site.

Strengths
Internal/Positive

Recognized brand
Impressive product line

Weaknesses
Internal/Negative

Under staffed
Lack of experience

Opportunities
External/Positive

Expanding customer base
Growing industry

Threats
External/Negative

Strong competition
Economic factors

The result of a client briefing and customer interviews is a project or creative brief. A *creative brief* outlines the goals for a project, the special considerations the team must take in order to complete the project effectively, as well as a schedule of milestone events. A brief is usually reviewed by the team and the client and signed off, forming the directional foundation for the project.

(Opposite) This creative brief template helps clients synthesize the goals of a project in a way that can help remove a lot of the subjectivity that comes with creative projects.

(Below) A Gantt chart shows the timing of the tasks involved in a project in relationship to one another, helping the team see the big picture.

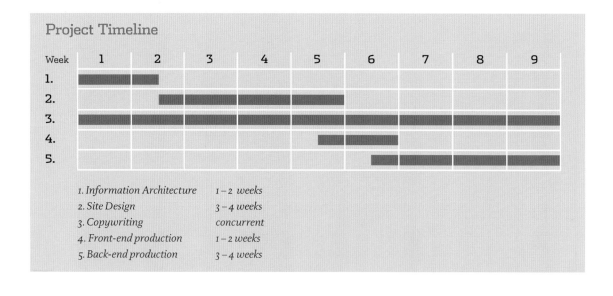

Project Timeline

Week	1	2	3	4	5	6	7	8	9
1.									
2.									
3.									
4.									
5.									

1. *Information Architecture*   *1 – 2 weeks*
2. *Site Design*   *3 – 4 weeks*
3. *Copywriting*   *concurrent*
4. *Front-end production*   *1 – 2 weeks*
5. *Back-end production*   *3 – 4 weeks*

Creative Brief

Project Name:

Date:

Prepared by:

Submitted to:

Project Overview:

Background information:

Target user insight information:

Brand attributes, promise, and mission:

Competitive landscape:

Business objectives – success criteria:

Testing requirements – measurement of success:

Creative strategies:

Functionality and technical specifications:

Contribution and approval process:

Timelines:

Budget:

This fact-based portion of the brief should be concise and only include information pertaining to the desired outcome of this specific project.

The business objective should identify a single testing metric that drives the creative strategy and the decision-making process for the project

Defining the number of rounds of revisions and identifying a single point of contact (client and creative) will cause clients to focus their comments and streamline the process

Asset Inventory

A Web site design project can often be overwhelming at the beginning. There are many considerations to be made and items to be collected before designing can begin. Project assets like client logos, copy, images, and code libraries must all be identified and located. This process begins with an inventory of all the assets needed for a project—in other words, what are the elements of a site that the team will need to complete the project? This information can be collected in a spreadsheet, drawn out on a whiteboard, or sorted on index cards— whatever will produce the most comprehensive results. This process can be done by the creative team in parallel with the conduction of other phases by the information architecture and user experience teams.

Web design projects can be overwhelming at the start. Checklists, like the one seen here, help a designer run down the list of requirements for a project and reminds him or her of the critical needs.

Content Checklist

Copy

- ☐ Who will provide copy?
- ☐ Is there a budget for a copywriter?
- ☐ What are the copy mandatories?
- ☐ What's the correct tone for the audience and brand?

Imagery & Artwork

- ☐ Is there existing imagery? If yes, what format and resolution is it?
- ☐ Is there a budget for a photo shoot?
- ☐ Is there a stock photo budget?
- ☐ Are any custom illustrations needed?

Code

- ☐ What code can be reused, if any?
- ☐ Does this require custom programming or an off-the-shelf solution?
- ☐ Will there be a content management system (CMS)?
- ☐ Who will manage the content?

File Organization & Naming

A designer's ability to organize his or her working and production files is always important, but with Web design it's critical. This is because the files that a designer uses to create a site are the same files that a user will download and view on his or her computer. Factors such as file name, file type, file size, and directory organization are all significantly more important than with print design. HTML files reference other files with relative paths, which means they find other files based on their own location. Therefore, files need to be organized in clearly labeled directories, as seen in the diagram to the right.

Properly naming files can help improve workflow and, more importantly, ensure the files will be handled properly by the Web server. Rule number one is never use spaces in file names. While Mac and Windows systems can handle spaces with no issue, servers running UNIX can have difficulty with spaces.

Clear file names help the programmer understand the content of the file and they help organize the directories for a Web site. The example file names seen here are all buttons, thus they start with "btn_" and because of this they group together alphabetically. Note that they're all lowercase as well. This is for consistency and because some languages like XML and XHTML are case sensitive, so to be safe designers should stick with an all-lowercase convention.

Main Directory

HTML/CSS files

Image directory

Javascript directory

Media directory

btn_red.gif
btn_blue.gif
btn_green.gif
btn_orange.gif

Sitemap

The information architecture phase of a Web site project usually starts with the development of a comprehensive *sitemap*. A sitemap is a schematic for a site showing the pages and the linked relationships among them. Traditionally, pages are represented by outlined boxes, and links are represented by lines connecting the boxes. This document gives a design team an overview of the site and allows designers to understand the breadth of the navigational needs and the full scope of the project: What pages are most important? What pages need to be reached from every page? Is there a target page that the client wants to lead people to? All of these questions can be answered by examining a sitemap.

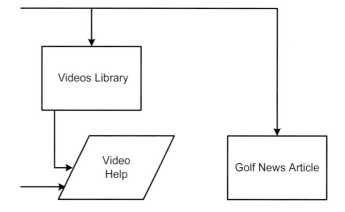

A sitemap, like the one shown here for GolfersMD.com, shows the pages of a site and their relationship to one another. Pages are laid out and grouped by the information architect, showing various pathways and connections that a design team uses when laying out the navigation and sub-navigation. In this case, the items in the main navigation are shaded in blue, pages that require the user to log in are shaded in gray, and pop-up windows are slanted boxes.

The sitemap on the next page illustrates that even a very large and seemingly unwieldy site becomes more manageable when neatly organized by an information architect.

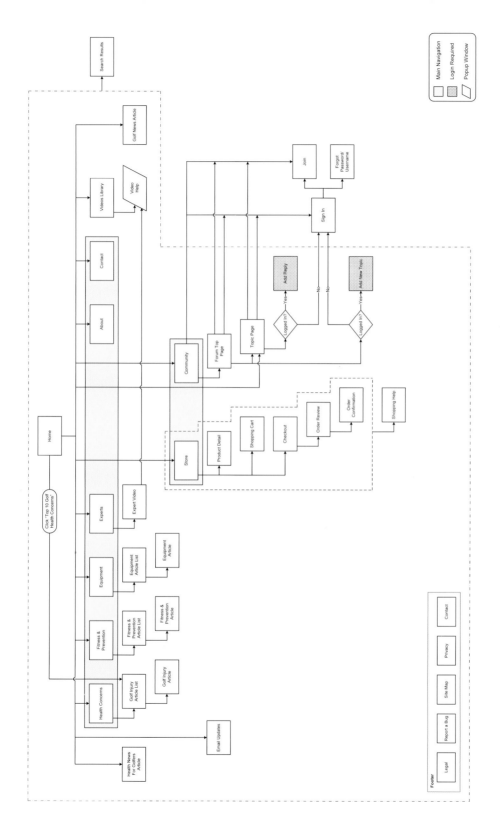

Site Planning

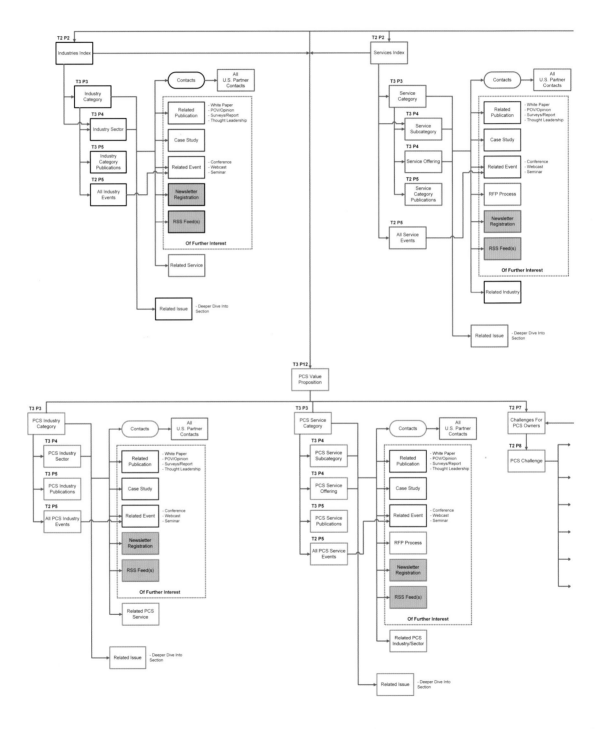

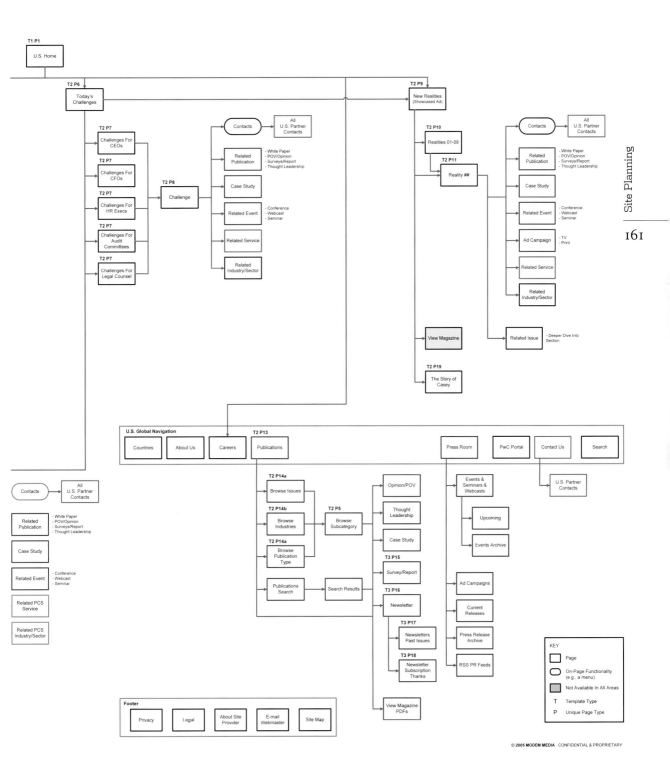

Wireframes are **blueprints** that map out individual pages of a site. They show the elements of a page and their relative weight or importance.

Wireframe

Wireframes are blueprints that map out individual pages. The wireframe shows the elements of a page and their relative weight or importance. They are not intended to lay out the page; instead, they give a designer an idea of what the most important elements are, what the second most important elements are, and so on. Wireframes can be made for any page of the site that needs detail. The home page, subpage templates, registration forms, search results, or any page that needs clarification can be wireframed for the designer.

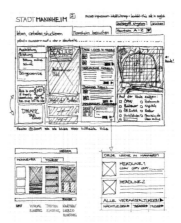

The wireframes seen here and on the next spread are what user experience experts and information architects use to organize a page for a design team. Wireframes are the bones that a designer uses to flesh out by adding brand elements and aesthetic treatments.

| Logo | _SITE NAME_ | | Welcome, Swhite | Settings | Help | Logout |

Tuesday, February 20, 2007   Find a Colleague ▽ | Browse By Tag ▽ | [ ] Search

| Home | Blog | Prof. Development | Knowledge Resources | Marketing Excellence | My Profile

In The Spotlight

Nike to Change Shopping Experience

Nike wants to change the way consumers shop!

"Consumers want a more compelling and relevant experience wherever and whenever they shop," Nike President and Chief Executive Mark Parker said.

Discuss on the Blog >

Latest Blog Post

Sterling Hayden on Feb 20, 2007:

Integer consequat. Sed sed lacus. Aliquam erat volutpat. Pellentesque facilisis urna quis odio. Curabitur rhoncus.

Aliquam erat. Donec at libero vel mi dignissim accumsan. Nam ante tellus, porta ut, sollicitudin id. Nullam fermentum luctus leo...

Go To Post >

Featured Content

| **Campaigns** | Knowledge Base |

5th Anniversary of Volvo's awards program honoring America's favorite hometown heroes.

Campaign: "Volvo For Life"
Media: TV, Online, Print, Event

Go To Campaign >

| News | Clip Sheets | Select Feeds ▽

News: All Topics   Search News ▽

| **Most Recent** | Most Viewed | Top Rated | All Stories |

- **10 Secrets of Successful Online Community**
  Tue Feb 20, 2007 02:37 PM (_SOURCE_)
  Views: 128,234   ☆☆☆☆☆ Avg. Rating (0 votes)   Tags: _TAG NAME_, _TAG NAME_

- **The Ultimate Social Network You Haven't Heard Of**
  Tue Feb 20, 2007 01:54 PM (_SOURCE_)
  Views: 536   ★★★☆☆ Avg. Rating (498 votes)   Tags: _TAG NAME_

  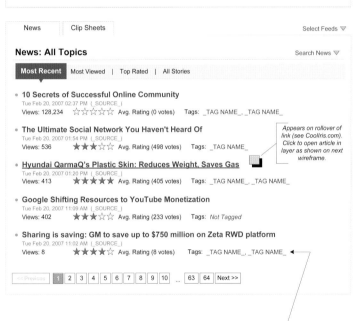

  Appears on rollover of link (see CoolIris.com). Click to open article in layer as shown on next wireframe.

- <u>**Hyundai QarmaQ's Plastic Skin: Reduces Weight, Saves Gas**</u>
  Tue Feb 20, 2007 01:20 PM (_SOURCE_)
  Views: 413   ★★★★★ Avg. Rating (405 votes)   Tags: _TAG NAME_, _TAG NAME_

- **Google Shifting Resources to YouTube Monetization**
  Tue Feb 20, 2007 11:09 AM (_SOURCE_)
  Views: 402   ★★★☆☆ Avg. Rating (233 votes)   Tags: *Not Tagged*

- **Sharing is saving: GM to save up to $750 million on Zeta RWD platform**
  Tue Feb 20, 2007 11:02 AM (_SOURCE_)
  Views: 8   ★★★★☆ Avg. Rating (8 votes)   Tags: _TAG NAME_, _TAG NAME_ ◄

| <<Previous | 1 | 2 | 3 | 4 | 5 | 6 | 7 | 8 | 9 | 10 | ... | 63 | 64 | Next >> |

If there is a premium on space and a desire to display more headlines above the fold, consider NOT showing the "Views, Rating, Tag" line. The values are implicit in the filtering choices on the top bar and via the Tags option in the Search News dropdown. They are also explicitly displayed when the article is opened.

BuzzMetrics Stats

Brand: [Volvo ▼]

Total identified blogs: **42,192,419**

New blogs in last 24 hours: **66,477**

Blog posts indexed in last 24 hours: **503,650**

Go To Report >

Events Calendar

| 04-04-2007 | Ford Marketing Conference | New York, NY USA |
| 04-24-2007 | Advertising Age: Marketing In The Digital Age | London, England UK |

See Full Calendar >

Suggestions For The Site?

Have some great content and feature ideas for the site? Discuss them in the Site Suggestions blog.

Usability Diagrams

Usability diagrams (also known as user-flow diagrams or use cases) combine a sitemap and a wireframe to plan out a specific action a user might take on a site, and the process of how it occurs. For example, to show how someone might register on a site, a usability diagram would show a home page, a registration page that's linked from the home page, an error page showing that the user didn't complete all the required fields, a "thank you" page showing the registration was complete, and a confirmation email wireframe. User-flow diagrams show every step of the process and can help uncover potential issues. The process of creating a use case can be as valuable as the resulting diagram. The exercise of acting as a user and imagining interaction with the site is a critical preparation step in designing for the Web.

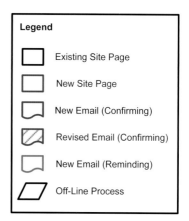

The usability diagram seen here goes a step beyond a sitemap and illustrates the path a user might take through a site. The diagram can include not only on-site pages, but emails and even off-site actions like going to a retail store or calling an 800 number. These help the Web project team lead the user to the intended goal of the client in the most effective way.

On-Boarding Flow

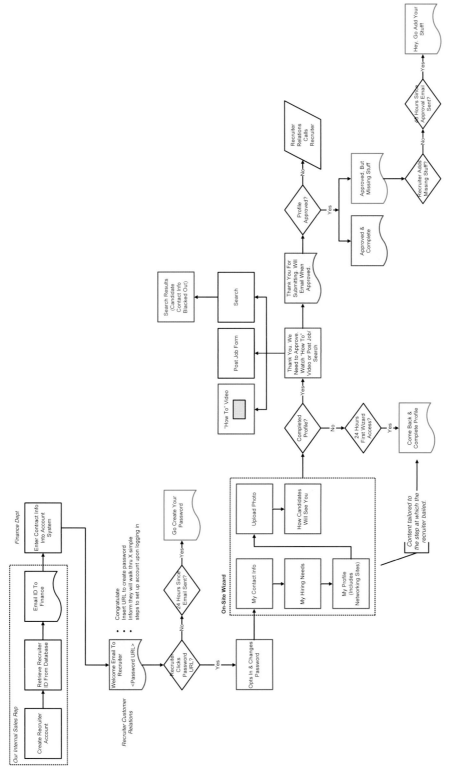

Prototypes are working models of site functionality that help a developer work out the final details and provide **proof of concept.**

Prototypes

Once the wireframing is complete and critical tasks are mapped out, it's sometimes necessary to create *functional prototypes* for new or complicated functionality. Prototypes are working models of site features or functionality that help a developer and a designer work out the final details and provide proof of concept. These working models, which are usually void of any design treatment, provide valuable opportunities for evaluation and refinement that can't be done with diagrams alone. Once a prototype is functional, it's ready to be "skinned" by the designer. *Skinning* is a term used by designers that means to add a design treatment on top of a working model.

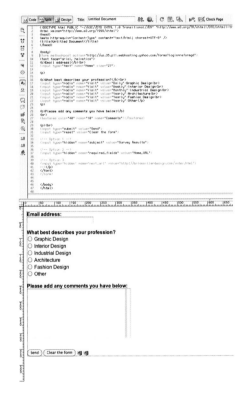

Prototypes, like the ones seen here, are created by the development team to flesh out specific technological challenges and to create a proof of concept that an idea can actually be executed.

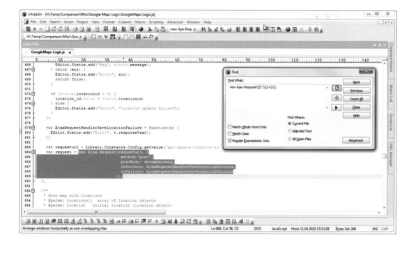

Functionality development can take a lot of trial and error before it's ready for deployment. This back-and-forth process can often yield valuable testing data that can help both the design and usability teams.

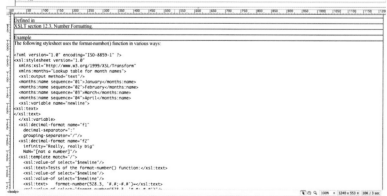

Concept Design

The final pre-design step for most designers is the concept phase. In this phase a designer or design team might create what's called a *moodboard*. Moodboards collect the brand assets, like logos and product photography, and mix them with stylistic photography or illustrations, a color palette, bits of copy, and any other elements that can give a client a sense of the creative direction. These layouts aren't intended to look like a Web site at all; instead, they're abstract compositions with a focus on an aesthetic feel. Several moodboards might be created and presented to the client for approval prior to beginning the design phase.

The moodboards seen here created by the Wonderfactory help a client get a feel for the visual mood of a site prior to seeing the finished design, also seen here.

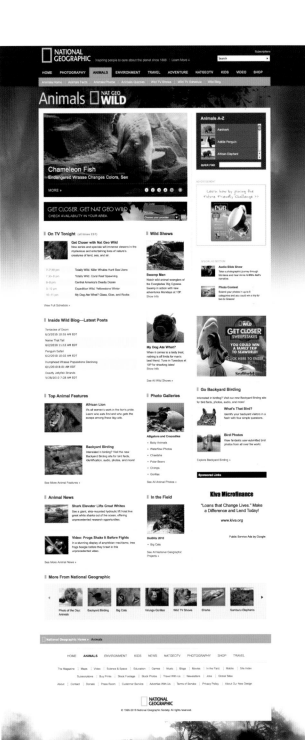

CHAPTER 7

ELEMENTS OF USABILITY

Usability is a term that refers to the ease with which users can learn, engage with, and get satisfaction, from an interface for a Web site or piece of software. While the usability diagrams are helpful for a designer to plan out a Web site, usability effectiveness also comes from a variety of other factors from design, server speed, technology usage, animation, and even sound effects. This chapter explores the following interface elements, which, when combined, cover the usability touchpoints for a user: navigation, breadcrumbs, site search, submission forms, text links, and error messages. While usability comes from more than just these interface elements, these are the features of a site that a designer can most greatly influence. The examples shown in this chapter demonstrate various means of effectively joining design and usability.

Elements of Usability

Enough About You

Usability is about the user. Usability is directly related to the experience a user has with a site—the better the usability, the better the experience is likely to be. Individual users vary widely, even within a single target market. In Web design, standard demographic data such as age, education, gender, language, interests, and culture apply—but there's an added level of demographic information that includes information about technology, like operating system, processor speed, screen resolution, memory, and network connection speed. All of this demographic information can play an influential role when it comes to usability design.

Usability is such a critical aspect of Web design that many Web design agencies employ user experience (UX) experts. Part sociologist, part technician, this person is responsible for determining the most appropriate usability based on the abilities and expectations of the target user group, as well as the technology that's available. There is no one "right" way to design the usability features of a site. Some factors that influence the level of usability include:

- The purpose of a site: Is the site meant to be fun or strictly business?
- The needs and experience level of the user: How computer savvy is he or she?
- The technology that's available: Is there new technology that could make finding information easier?

Navigation

Navigation is a broad term that encompasses any aspect of a site that links a user to another area of the site and is the cornerstone of a site's usability. Unlike other forms of information design that have a natural sequence—pages of a book or brochure, for example—Web pages present users with a menu of options and allow them to chose their own order. The main navigation of a site is the primary set of links that a user clicks to get to the important content of a site. The most common convention for main navigation is a persistent bar across the upper part of a page that features a list of five to seven options, with other options relegated to subnavigation. (Groups of five to seven are generally what people are capable of perceiving before attempting to break them down into subgroups.)

There are two ways of dealing with large site architectures: Categorize content into main sections, then use a cascading system of menus either with drop-down lists or sub-menus; or break up the list of choices into the most important items (primary navigation) and the lesser important items (secondary navigation). In either case, six groups of five are much easier to comprehend than one group of thirty. Either method makes comprehending the site architecture easier for the user and reduces the number of clicks it takes for a user to get from one place on the site to another.

These images show the drop-down menu navigation on newyorkmag.com. Information is grouped into six main categories for greater usability.

CustomToronto.ca has both a horizontal main navigation and a vertical sub-navigation. Items are grouped in numbers of five or six.

ExpressionEngine.com uses an inverted dimensional tab system along with illustrative icons for the main feature selections. The large, clear buttons make selecting a feature easy.

Navigational elements need to visually stand apart from the rest of the elements on the page and indicate that the user can click on them. There are usually four states to an item in a navigation bar: the dormant or static state; the active state, which indicates the current page; a rollover state, which is sometimes the same as the active state when a user mouses over the button; and the visited state, which indicates to the user what's already been visited. This system should be easy for the user to learn and should remain consistent throughout the entire site.

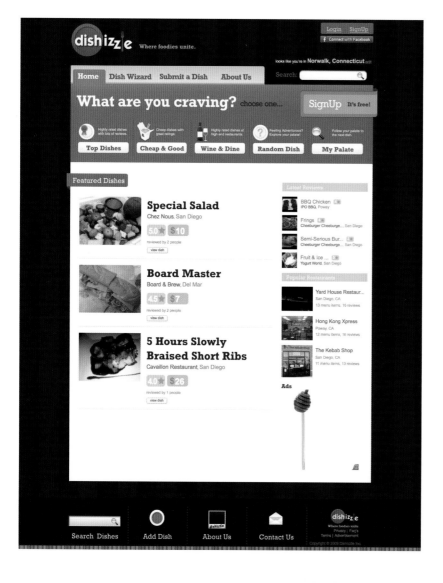

Dishizzle.com uses various types of buttons for various types of navigation: tabs for the main navigation, buttons for features, a flag for the signup link, icons in the footer, as well as clearly identifiable text links.

The language of a button should clearly and accurately predict the content of the destination page. The labels should be written from the user's perspective, with terms users might use to find what they're looking for. (Users are quick to abandon a site if they have been confused or deceived by a misleading button.) In addition, since search engines often value the text within links, it's important to use keyword-rich terms in the navigation. This is also why the most effective navigation bars use Web fonts for the buttons—not images of text, which are unreadable by search engines.

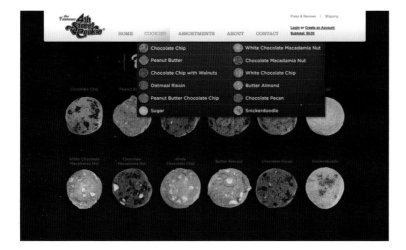

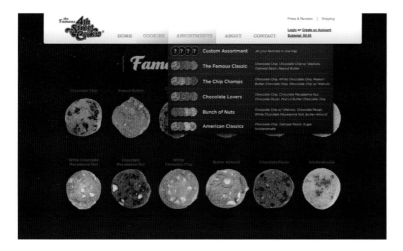

The drop-down menu on FamousCookies.com has not only descriptive copy but small imagery of cookies, making finding the right section easier.

Breadcrumbs

A useful subset of navigation is something called *breadcrumb links* or *breadcrumbs.* Breadcrumb links reveal to the user the path taken through the site architecture to get to the current page, thus making it easier to go back. The name *breadcrumbs* comes from the story of Hansel and Gretel, when Hansel scattered crumbs of bread on the ground to help him and his sister find their way home. Unfortunately for the pair, birds came along and ate their breadcrumbs, but the metaphor lives on as a trail of tasty links guiding users on Web sites.

A form of breadcrumbing is also used for submission forms. An indicator bar is sometimes used across the top of a form to reveal the number of steps in the process—both what they've completed as well as the steps yet to come. This helps estimate how long a submission form is and whether it's worth the user's time to complete.

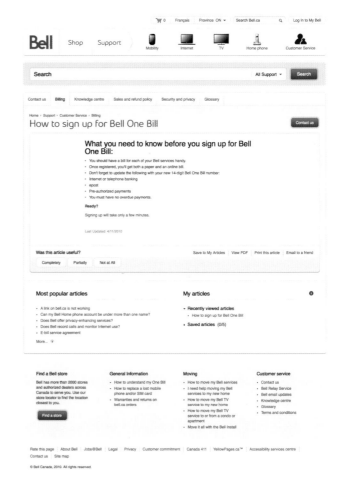

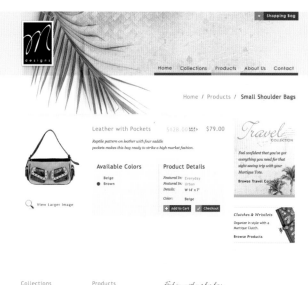

Breadcrumb links like those seen in these samples act as a sub-navigation that light a user's way back to the home page.

Breadcrumbs can be simple links or more elaborate drop-down menus like the ones seen above. In both cases they help the user ground himself or herself on the site.

Text Links

Within the content of a site, it's often necessary to link users to other areas of the site for additional content. This granular level of navigation is helpful to users who want to know more about a specific idea, and helpful for SEO because linked words have high indexing value. Since linked text usually consists of keywords from the article, highlighting the links helps the "scanability" of a page—a user can scan and read the linked words and get a general sense for the content of the page. Links in long bodies of text, however, can also be a distraction to a user who's trying to focus on a single story. For this reason, links should stand out so they can be recognized, but not so much so that they're distracting.

These examples from AndyRutledge.com (top) and JustWatchTheSky.com (below) show alternate ways to highlight links. Any CSS style variation is possible when indicating links, from underlining and color changes to size, weight, and background color shifts.

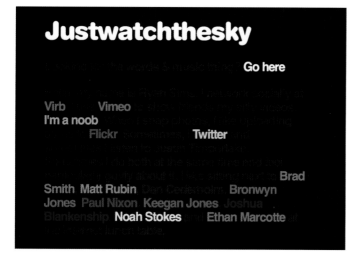

According to leading usability authority Jakob Nielsen (useit.com), the best method for indicating a text link is underlining and changing the color of linked text; however, any alteration is available when indicating a link in CSS. Aside from the indication of a link, there should also be two other visual states of a link: mouse over and visited. The mouse over state gives the user visual feedback that the text is indeed a link and not just underlined for emphasis. The visited state helps the user recognize where he or she has been. There's also a less common active state, which appears the moment a user clicks.

Site Search

Perhaps the quickest way to allow users to find information on a Web site is through a site search feature. Search forms search a database of site content and display the results for a user, linking them directly to the item they came for—ideally. Because a search box is intended to increase usability, it should be as easy to find and use as possible. This means placing it above the fold in a conspicuous location that's consistent on every page and clearly labeled "Search" or something similar. Also, it's important to make the search field long enough to accommodate the types of searches people will conduct. Although longer search terms can be entered into a short field, users tend to edit themselves if they're given a small space. It is also possible to pre-populate the search form with the type of search available by the form.

Internal site searches will sometimes have an advanced search feature. This is an extension of the search functionality with added fields that allow a user to narrow down a search to increase the likelihood of finding what is needed. The most effective search boxes have the ability to remember popular searches and match them to the characters entered by the user so the user can see, then click on, a list of potential search terms and be redirected to those results.

The search features on Typography.com, which includes "find fonts" and "browse collections" drop-down features, make finding content on the site easy and intuitive.

Usability Testing

While creative focus groups can be the death of fresh ideas, usability testing, which consists of inviting potential users to complete a series of tasks using the interface concept, can greatly help refine the usability elements of a site. During a usability test session, the moderator observes and records the users' reactions and emotions as they attempt to complete a given task. Confusion or frustration expressed by the user help pinpoint trouble spots, whereas delight or satisfaction means that the usability is appropriate for the task and the user.

To the right is a sample transcript from a usability test. In this example the subject tester is asked to find books about graphic design. The moderator prompts the user with tasks and nothing more. The users actions and quotes are recorded and the icons indicate positive or negative feedback, as well as feedback that represents an idea by the user.

First impressions

"I like the design and the colors, but I don't know where to begin. I suppose if I had something to do here I would know where to start."

Please search for information about graphic design books.
Subject starts search

"The search field is a bit short, which makes me think I can only search for single terms."

Subject receives 18 results.

"It would be great if these results could be sorted by price and availability."

Subject really likes the layout of the results page, including the thumbnail images of the books.

Please select a book for purchase
Subject clicks the thumbnail of the book to view detail and nothing happens.

"I should be able to click the image of the book to see the product descriptions."

Subject clicks "Learn More" and sees product description page.

"I like this page, but it's too hard to find the price. I want to know immediately how much this book costs."

Subject adds book to shopping cart.

"I like how I don't leave the page when the book is added to the cart."

Subject clicks the "Check Out" link and proceeds to check out page.

The search field is only half of a
site search solution; the **search
results page** is the other.

The search field is only half of a site search
solution; the search results page is the other.
There are a couple of important features of
a results page that can help with usability.
The searched term should remain in the
search box at the top of the page and the
number of results found should also clearly
be displayed. Effective search results pages
give users the ability to sort the results—by
date, by relevance, or by author, for example.
The search results themselves should display
enough key information so the user can
make an informed decision as to whether the
results are the desired ones. Finally, on the
article page, there should be a mechanism
that allows users to rate the relevance and
quality of the article based on the user's
search criteria. This will teach the search
engines what content is most relevant for
different search terms.

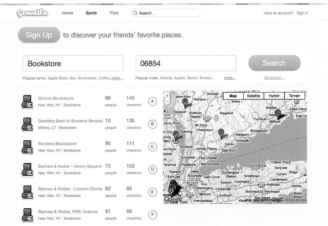

(Left, top) The search results on Gap.com feature photos of the clothing related to the search by the user. This makes finding and selecting the right items easier.

(Left, bottom) GoWalla.com does a good job at making it clear to the user what he or she has searched and displaying the search results in both list form and map locations.

(This page) Etsy.com has a very clean top navigation with an equally intuitive search feature. The search area starts with a drop down menu of categories, followed by a search field that offers popular search suggestions based on the letters a user types in. The search results (bottom) are sortable and can be converted from image view to list view.

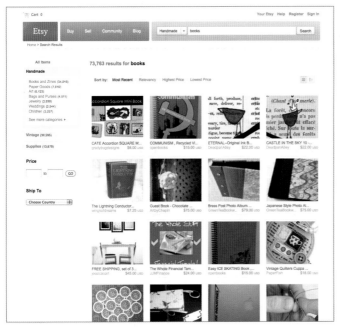

As a general rule, users don't like filling out forms, so it's the job of the designer and UX specialist to make the process as **pain-free** as possible.

Submission Forms

Submission forms, where a user inputs information and submits it to the site, generally represent a goal for a site—inviting the user to register, sign up for a newsletter, buy a product—so the usability of a submission form is of premium importance. Unfortunately, as a general rule, users don't like filling out forms, so it's the job of the designer and UX specialist to make the process as pain-free as possible. It's important to be clear about the length of the form up front, with long forms broken up into manageable segments with a breadcrumb trail indicating what's left to come.

A form is a series of fields that a user fills out with information. The fields should be clearly labeled with the information that needs to go in them. Designing the labels to the left of the field, as opposed to above them, will give the appearance of a shorter form. Required and optional fields should be indicated clearly so the user knows what fields can be skipped. Fields should be grouped in a logical way so the user can follow the flow easily, and redundant information, such as shipping versus billing information, should be pre-populated if the user desires. When validation (an available username, for example) is required, it should be given in process, not after the form has been submitted. The number of times a user has to correct errors and resubmit a form greatly increases the likelihood that the user will drop off.

It's often useful for a designer to limit the number of actions a user can take when on a form page. This can mean removing all global navigation and limiting the clickable options to "Submit" and possibly some "Help" links. After submitting a form, a user should be given a clear indication that the submission was successful.

CONTACT

Adding style to a submission form can make it more inviting for the user. The forms seen here, from the simple email form above to the more complex content management forms on the opposite page, benefit from a clear grid, generous white space, and typographic hierarchy.

These form examples from Threadless.com (top) and ColabFinder.com (bottom) utilize an underlying grid structure to organize the space in the layout, which helps minimize the appearance of large amounts of information to fill in.

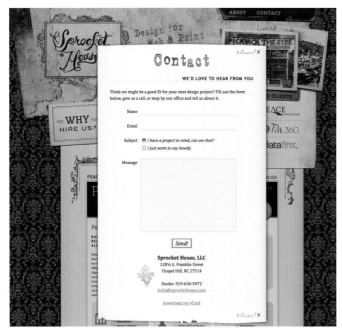

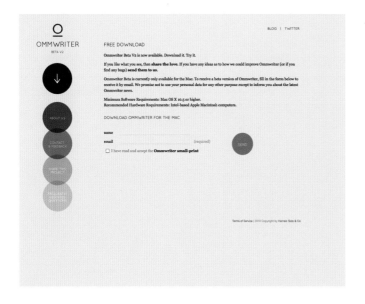

These form examples from SprocketHouse.com (top) and OmmWriter.com (bottom) style the form elements in a way that causes them to blend in with the design. Although rarely taken advantage of, CSS can style form fields just like any other element within a design.

Each **form element** has a specific purpose that a designer should understand when designing an online form.

This sample form shows the various form elements that are used to collect information. Each element has a specific purpose that a designer should understand when designing an online form.

There are three types of text fields: textbox collects a single line of information; textbox with password protection collects a single line of information but the user only sees bullets or asterisks; and textarea, which can collect multiple lines of text. Text fields can be set to be pre-populated with a phrase to help the user understand the type of information that can be input.

For selecting items there are three main choices: radio buttons (seen as circles in this diagram) are mutually exclusive—meaning only one can be selected from a group—and they allow for written explanations of the options; drop-down menus are also mutually exclusive and they provide a simple list of items; and checkboxes (seen as boxes in this diagram), which are used for allowing the user to select multiple options.

The submit button triggers the action of a form and can either be a browser-generated user interface (UI) element, an image, or text.

Form Title

Input 1

Password

Input 2

⦿ **Option 1**
Single-line description copy for option 1

◯ **Option 2**
Single-line description copy for option 2

◯ **Option 3**
Single-line description copy for option 3

Selection 1

| Select ▼ |

Selection 2

☒ Choice 1

☐ Choice 2

Action

Error Messages

Despite the best efforts of designers and UX experts, users will sometimes come across an error on a site. The most common errors on submission forms occur when the proper information is not filled in correctly. Indicating an error clearly can be essential in converting users who are willing to spend time filling out a form. To clearly indicate an error, a designer should visually separate the error message from the page so the user easily notices it. The content of the message should be clear yet polite, and the offending form should be highlighted clearly so the user can find it quickly and make the correction.

This example from OnSugar. com is not an error, but a hint that appears as the user selects the various form fields. This proactive approach can help reduce the need for error messaging altogether.

The example error messages here from PopScreen.com clearly identify the fields that need to be corrected as well as the error that has occurred.

In the lower example on this page— barleysgville.com—the error message is displayed as a single line below the form, with a list of the missed fields.

These examples range from subtle markings to obvious red fields and caution icons. The right level of strength for the error message depends as much on the layout environment it appears in as the experience level of the user group that will be using the site.

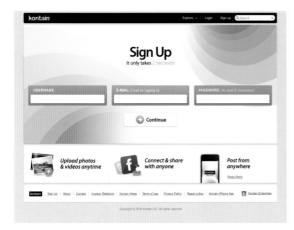

"Something went technically wrong.
Thanks for noticing—we're going to fix it up and have things back to normal soon."

The right copy can play an important role in effective error messaging, since it's easy for the user to feel like he or she has done something wrong. In this example from Twitter.com, the copy reads, "Something went technically wrong. Thanks for noticing—we're going to fix it up and have things back to normal soon."

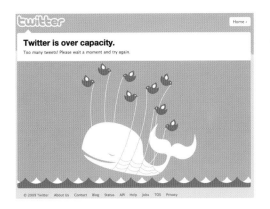

The "Fail Whale," also from Twitter.com, is a surprising yet delightful error message. The unexpected nature of a whale being flown by birds makes finding an error almost forgivable.

The surprising number of hits a 404 page receives makes it a **prime design opportunity** to direct the user and reinforce the client's brand.

Another form of error message is the "404 Page Not Found." Often overlooked by designers, this page appears when a user lands on a URL that no longer exists or never existed. The surprising number of hits a 404 page gets makes it a prime design opportunity to direct the user and reinforce the client's brand. Custom 404 pages should be somewhat apologetic in tone and present a series of links so the user can find what he or she originally was looking for. The ability to search or even report the missing page is an additional feature that can be added to a 404 page.

This custom 404 page from Heinz.com combines both an element of humor with the utility of being able to find information on the site.

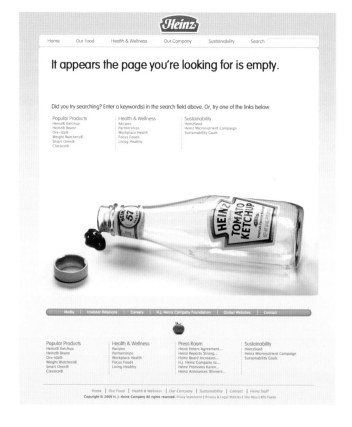

Surprise and Delight

While the Web has many utilitarian aspects to it, it's also important to remember that users—people—enjoy being entertained. "Surprise and delight" is a phrase adopted from the hospitality industry and used by Web designers and UX specialists to describe the fun or unexpected features of a site. (This should not be confused with "mislead and confuse.") Surprise and delight refers to added value for a user—something that goes beyond expectations. Surprise and delight can be humorous, irreverent, or even seductive. Exactly what kind of surprise is appropriate, like anything else, depends on the target audience.

The 404 pages seen here and on the next spread are prime examples of surprise and delight.

These custom 404 pages from ILoveTypography.com (top) and teez.com.au (center and bottom) illustrate a sense of the company's brands, both with a sense of beauty and humor.

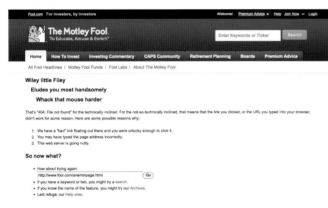

The custom 404 pages on this page from Sony.com (top), Fool.com (center), and InspirationBit.com (bottom) have both a sense of brand but also provide a means for the user to find the content he or she was seeking—from a site nav and links to a search field.

Traffic Sources Overview

May 28, 2010 - Jun 27, 2010 ▾

All traffic sources sent a total of 12,331 visits

36.56% Direct Traffic

35.52% Referring Sites

27.92% Search Engines

■ **Direct Traffic**
4,508.00 (36.56%)
■ **Referring Sites**
4,380.00 (35.52%)
■ **Search Engines**
3,443.00 (27.92%)

Top Traffic Sources

Sources	Visits	% visits
(direct) ((none))	4,508	36.56%
google (organic)	3,302	26.78%
facebook.com (referral)	287	2.33%
twitter.com (referral)	267	2.17%
siteinspire.net (referral)	255	2.07%

view full report

Keywords	Visits	% visits
tdc	772	22.42%
type directors club	624	18.12%
tdc.org	99	2.88%
type designers club, new york	95	2.76%
ny tdc	42	1.22%

view full report

BUSINESS VALUE

Search Engine Optimization
Marketing & Conversion
Analysis

CHAPTER 8

SEARCH ENGINE OPTIMIZATION

So far, this book has focused on the designer and the user, but there's a third leg to the Web design stool: the client. Clients are always looking for the maximum financial return possible on their Web project investment. Return on investment (ROI) is critical because developing a Web site can be quite expensive and organizations need to show value for the money they invest in a Web project. While design plays an enormous role in building a strong brand and well-thought-out usability gives customers a great experience, neither matters if the target audience cannot find a site. Attracting the maximum possible number of site visitors is essential for the success of a site—and, in turn, the success of the company that owns the site. Simply put, getting found is everything to a business.

Getting Discovered: Browsing and Searching

There are three primary ways a user finds a specific site: by typing an address (URL) directly into the browser address bar; by browsing and following links or advertisements from one site to another; or by searching a topic in a search engine such as Google. While there's some debate over this topic, most research shows that well over half of Internet users start by searching a topic using a search engine. This chapter explores the considerations one must make while planning, designing, coding, and promoting a site so search engines can find and index it.

Just like with Web design and Web usability, search engine optimization (SEO) is continually evolving based on trends and market factors. It would be difficult to codify specific techniques in a book whose usefulness is intended to last beyond the publish date. Therefore, this chapter focuses on the conceptual foundation of SEO—the basic principles that form the core of various trends. The exact techniques for a specific market or site can easily be found, ironically, by searching the Web for SEO. Understanding why SEO is important, and the basic principles that influence effective results, help a designer approach the planning and creation of a site with the correct mindset.

Types of Search Engines

There are two types of search engines:

Crawler based, like Bing.com and Google.com, which find sites using spiders to crawl the Web and index content. A spider is a software tool that seeks out heavily trafficked servers for popular sites. Spiders are programmed to follow every link within a site all while indexing the words it finds on each page. Crawler-based search engines gather information about a site and rank that site based on a series of on-site and external factors that will be explored in this chapter.

Directories, such as dmoz.org, rely on volunteer editors to evaluate sites for a specific topic and determine whether they should be listed in the directory. While these types of directories provide highly relevant sites, the process of selecting sites can be slow, which can result some newer sites not appearing in the directory. Directory sites, however, can provide significant SEO value to a site that is listed with them. The inbound links (IBL) from popular directories to a site help to dramatically raise that site's ranking with crawler-based search engines.

It's important to remember that many Internet users are not at all tech savvy, and depending on the target demographic of a specific site, this could be the majority of users. In fact, in an amusing (and completely unscientific) YouTube video* produced by Google, fewer than eight percent of people interviewed knew the difference between a browser and a search engine—most thought they were one and the same. For the sake of clarity in this chapter,

Top Crawler-Based Search Engines

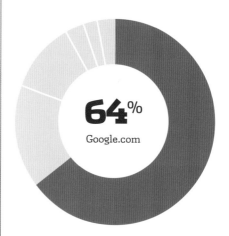

Google	64%
Yahoo!	16%
Bing	11%
AOL Search	3%
Ask	2%
Other	3%

Source: Nielsen MegaView Search

Just like with Web design and Web usability, search engine optimization (SEO) techniques are **continually evolving** based on trends and market factors.

Google™

bing™

YAHOO!®

Google, Yahoo!, and Bing are the three most widely used crawler-based search engines on the Internet.

a browser is an application installed on the user's computer and is used to browse and display Web pages. Some popular browsers are Internet Explorer, Safari, and Firefox. A search engine is a Web site or Web utility that catalogs sites, through various means, and presents the user with a list of sites that are relevant to their search. Some popular search engines are Google, Yahoo! and Bing. A browser requires the user to know the exact domain name or URL of a site, beginning with www. and ending with .com, .org, etc., while a search engine requires only that a user have a topic he or she would like to find out more about.

The goal of any search engine is to sort through the millions of Web sites on the Internet and deliver the most popular and relevant sites to a user based on a search term or phrase. The goal of a Webmaster is to stand out from the millions of sites and get his or her site listed however possible. It's an ever-evolving cat-and-mouse game where the rules change over time.

Early search engines relied mostly on site content when developing their rankings. A spider would simply read the text and the markup (the tags and code unseen by the user) to determine the content type and quality of a page. Some of these hidden bits of markup code include meta keywords, which can be listed in the <head> tag of the HTML and are intended to be the key terms and phrases used in the content of the page; the meta description, which is also found in the <head> tag and briefly describes the content of a page; and alt text (alternative text), which is a written description of a photo, for example, that can be translated to speech for vision-impaired users.

One issue with this method of cataloging is that these unseen tags can be filled with irrelevant terms that are nevertheless designed to yield high traffic. Say, for example, a Webmaster launched a site for a brand-new widget. It's unlikely that anyone would be searching for this widget, so he might load the meta tags with terms related to cars because he knows millions of people search for terms related to cars every day—even though his widget has nothing to do with cars. He may even put some white text talking about cars on his home page on a white background—white on white wouldn't be seen by the user but would be read as content by the spider. Within time, this widget site would begin appearing on searches for "cars," however, when a user clicked on the link looking for car information. The user would be disappointed to see that this site has no actual content related to cars—only widgets. This is called *spamdexing* or *Black Hat SEO*.

Additionally, as the Internet evolved through the 1990s and into the 2000s, so did the types of content on Web sites. So-called "rich media," such as Flash, audio, and video content, cannot be indexed by search engines using typical methods. Since spiders cannot listen to, watch, or interact with content, sites that employ rich content were not ranking.

Search engines quickly caught on and began adjusting their methods of ranking sites to reduce spam, detect Black Hat tactics, and increase the ranking of sites that employed rich media. While some search engines continue to employ a site's meta description as the brief blurb under the link on a search results page, meta descriptions are not weighted heavily when ranking the site. Nor are meta keywords, alt tags, or other elements not seen by the end user, because of the ease with which they can be manipulated. Instead, search engines now use a combination of a site's popularity, in addition to its content, to determine their rank for the site. To do this, search engines not only look at onsite elements like title tags—the text that appears in the top of the browser window—but also offsite factors like the domain name's age and links from other sites. In fact, offsite factors have a greater effect on a sites rank than do onsite factors. By effectively understanding which sites are the most popular in relation to specific search terms, search engines can reasonably ensure that the content is relevant to users who search those terms.

**Elements and Weight
of Google Ranking**

1. Trust in the Host Domain

2. Link Popularity

3. Anchor Text of External Links

4. On-Page Keyword Usage

5. Traffic and Click-Through Rate

6. Social Graph Metrics

7. Registration and Host Data

Source:: http://www.seomoz.org/article/search-ranking-factors

The Wild West

As search engines get more sophisticated in their methods of evaluating sites, so to do the individuals who intend to manipulate the results. A high search ranking can have a significant monetary value for an organization or an individual. As a result, the competition to reach the top with high-volume terms can get fierce. When money is involved, there's usually someone trying to cheat the system.

Honest, content-based methods of SEO, like those discussed in this chapter, are called White Hat techniques—*named for the good guys who always wore white in the Wild West movies. Conversely, Black Hat SEO tactics are deceitful and manipulative. Those who practice Black Hat SEO are generally looking for traffic volume for its own sake—not to entertain, inform, or in any way provide value to the user.*

Search engines retain the right to punish sites that practice Black Hat or deceitful tactics (knowingly or unknowingly) by removing them from their lists.

It's essential to select keywords based on the **customer's point of view**—not necessarily the client's internal vernacular.

Keywords

Before one can begin the process of implementing either onsite or external SEO techniques, one must first determine the best keywords for the site. Keywords are the specific terms that relate directly to the content of a site that people might use in their search. It's essential to select these terms based on the customer's point of view—not necessarily the client's point of view. Very often, clients speak of themselves using internal language—like product names or industry terms—that don't reflect how users search for information. It's important to understand how a user would define a client's business and use terms that fit their idea.

Users generally search for the solution to a problem they're experiencing: "What is [blank]?" "I need a [blank]," or "Where is [blank]?" Therefore, an effective strategy for developing a list of keywords is to position them as the answer to a question. These might be single words, but two-, three-, and even four-word phrases can be used. Identifying these words and phrases can involve a few methods.

Keyword tools such as the Google Keyword Tool, as well as third-party pay services, like WordTraker, help identify terms. These services are connected to a database of popular search terms and can cross-reference a specific term with other, synonymous terms that may have also been used to find sites related to the same topic. They can also provide information on the volume, popularity, and competition of terms as well.

Site indexing tools crawl a site and provide a list of the current keyword mix. This is a good place to start implementing an SEO strategy on an existing site.

(Opposite) This is a screenshot from the Google Keyword Tool. Searching the phrase "Web design books" produces the list of additional keyword ideas seen here. The list is helpful for determining the right balance of competition and monthly user searches—too much competition makes a word hard to target, yet too few monthly searches makes a word less than valuable.

Old-fashioned brainstorming, or roleplaying—"If I were a user, what would I search?"—can produce a valuable list of terms that can act as a starting point before using a keyword tool.

When developing a list of key terms or phrases, it's important to think of broad enough terms, so there's an adequate amount of search volume—but not so broad that there are so many results that competing for the top spot would be impossible. For example, imagine a site that sells golf shirts patterned after retro shirts from the 1950s. Simply using the term *golf* would be problematic, since there are roughly 292 million search results for the term *golf*—everything from golf clinics and clubs to golf vacations and books. However, the phrase *1950s golf shirts* is too specific and may not yield the search volume that the client is looking for. Therefore, phases like *classic golf shirts* or *buy retro shirts* might produce the right volume of qualified traffic with a reasonable ability to rank highly.

Keywords or phrases should not only accurately and specifically describe the content on a site; they should also be tailored to promoting conversion—a topic that's explored further in the next chapter. Most sites have a specific action they would like a user to take: sign up, buy, log in, etc. For these sites, it's not enough to simply be found—it's important to drive visitors who are looking to take action, so the keywords chosen for the site can include verbs like "buy," as in the previous example, to promote high-value traffic—not just high volume.

Keyword lists should be kept at a manageable length—25 to 75 words, depending on the size and type of site. A list that's too long can dilute the effectiveness of each individual keyword. Consistency and repetition is important for SEO, and a long list of words cuts down on the writer's ability to repeat terms. Although, it should be noted, some search engines may flag as spam a repetition of the exact same phrase numerous times, and this can be detrimental to a site's ranking. The terms that people use to search, and the concepts, ideas, and words used on a site evolve constantly—and therefore so should the list of SEO keywords. The list should be revisited frequently enough to be sure all of the terms are current and connected to the user.

Keyword ideas

Keyword	Competition	Global Monthly Searches	Local Monthly Searches	Local Search Trends
web design books		9,900	4,400	
web design page templates		110,000	74,000	
web design templates		74,000	40,500	
web page design		165,000	110,000	
web page design tutorial		14,800	6,600	
web page design software		90,500	60,500	
flash web page design		368,000	165,000	
web page design tools		33,100	18,100	
web design courses		49,500	18,100	
learn web design		9,900	6,600	
professional web page design		18,100	12,100	
web design tools		14,800	8,100	
sample web page design		12,100	6,600	
web graphic design		60,500	49,500	
web page design jobs		18,100	14,800	
web design layout		9,900	4,400	
freelance web designer		49,500	14,800	
learn web page design		4,400	3,600	
web page design ideas		2,900	1,900	
cool web page design		8,100	6,600	
web design studio		27,100	6,600	
web page design prices		6,600	4,400	
web design awards		18,100	9,900	
web design jobs		33,100	14,800	
web design company		201,000	90,500	
top web design		90,500	49,500	
flash web design		90,500	49,500	
web page design tips		3,600	1,600	
award winning web design		4,400	2,900	
web page design examples		12,100	6,600	
web page designer career		880	720	
custom web page design		22,200	14,800	
web design tutorial		27,100	9,900	
web design ideas		8,100	5,400	
personal web page design		49,500	40,500	
web design and development		90,500	40,500	
web page design cost		12,100	9,900	
web design software		165,000	74,000	
best web design		74,000	40,500	
good web design		12,100	6,800	
professional web design		60,500	33,100	
web design magazine		5,400	2,400	
great web design		5,400	2,900	
web design tips		12,100	5,400	
good web design examples		14,800	8,100	
artistic web design		720	590	
creative web design		22,200	8,100	
web design prices		27,100	14,800	
web design london		33,100	8,100	
web design services		110,000	60,500	

Designing for Spiders

Once a keyword list has been developed, it's time to begin employing those keywords on the site in ways that provide the most value for search engines. It's important to note that SEO factors shift in their overall importance, and no one factor will have a significant impact. It's the combination of these ideas and management of them over time that creates an effective SEO strategy.

When designing for SEO, it's important to remember the two most basic things about how a search engine ranks pages:
- Is this page what it claims to be?
- How popular is this page?

The former is done by highlighting—visually and technically—specific key phrases that describe the page. The latter is done by linking to the page, as we will discuss later in this chapter.

While the majority of SEO techniques center around developing content and establishing relationships with like-minded sites, designers can have an impact on the SEO value of a site. Designing for SEO means using Web-specific design methods, especially when it comes to displaying content, that yield visually interesting and dynamic results that search engines can index. This involves planning for an appropriate mix of graphics, animation, and content. Often, sites go too far toward one end of the spectrum or the other; too much of an SEO focus and a page can look generic or underdesigned, while too much of a design focus, such as over use of Flash or graphics for key text items, can result in poor search engine ranking. However, having an effectively optimized site doesn't mean it can't be designed well, and vice versa. It's simply a matter of employing the correct techniques.

The AIGA NY site employs many SEO best practices both seen and unseen. The site architecture is clear for easy crawling by spiders; links and headlines are filled with valuable keywords; and the source code is concisely written.

Designing for SEO means using **Web-specific design methods**, especially when it comes to displaying content, that yield visually interesting and dynamic results that search engines can index.

In previous chapters, this book explored the pros and cons of various means of displaying type—or, more accurately, content. Using methods to display "live" text (as opposed to images of text) is important, but the concept of designing for SEO goes beyond just using Web-safe type. The designer's arrangement of content is critical to effective SEO. Important, keyword-rich content should be displayed above the fold—the higher the better. The content should be broken up with headings and subheads, not only for scanability, but for SEO as well. Keyword-rich headings and subheadings should be styled using the "H" tags: <H1>, <H2>, <H3>, etc. The content in these tags are given greater weight by spiders since they are likely contain information about the key ideas on the page.

Having keywords above the fold for the user to see is important, but equally, if not more, important is having keywords appear as high as possible in the HTML code for the spiders to find. To do this, pages should be built using CSS and <div> tags rather than tables. Using tables, an older method of building page structures with rows and columns, results in longer code that can push down content in the markup. The CSS styling should be imported from an exterior CSS style sheet to avoid having long stretches of CSS code in the <head> tag of a page. The same is true for JavaScript functions, or anything that can unnecessarily lengthen the markup.

Images can play a role in SEO as well. Since images saved by a designer are the exact same images that get downloaded by the user for display in a browser, the file names are important. Keyword-rich file names can help SEO—widget.jpg instead of img_123.jpg, for example.

Arranging content and creating assets in a way that's both user friendly as well as spider friendly is a unique challenge for a Web designer. However, a designer can only have so much influence of the overall SEO strategy. An all-encompassing SEO strategy involves collaboration among a designer, a copywriter, the development team, the client, and even a media planner. What follows are other SEO factors that designers should be aware of, but often are the responsibility of others on the team.

To the right are excerpts from the code for the Web page seen on the far right, MillerWhiteSchool.org. Only some of the important SEO features are displayed here, including:

- Title tag, *which appears as part of the browser window above. It contains valuable keywords that users might search to find a school.*

- *The* meta description *is used by Google and other search engines to describe a site.*

- *The* meta keywords *are no longer heavily weighted by search engines but should be included nonetheless.*

- *The* navigation *is text based and filled with keywords.*

- *The H1 tag is actually the logo on the page. The text is indented off the visible page and replaced with a background image of the logo.*

- *Subheads are styled as* <H2> *tags.*

- *Body copy is filled with linked keywords.*

- *The* concluding link *also contains keywords rather than just "Learn more."*

<head>
<title>Graphic Design Classes and Workshops | The MillerWhite
School of Design</title>

<meta name="description" content="The MillerWhite School of
Design, located in Fairfield County, Connecticut, offers a program for
talented high school students interested in exploring the creative and
technical aspects of graphic design." />

<meta name="keywords" content="art school, norwalk, connecticut,
ct, art class, ct art school, graphic design, graphic design school,
graphic design program, graphic design class, art workshop,
graphic design training, graphic design course, graphic arts class,
fairfield county school, brian miller, brian d miller, alex white,
alexander white, alexander w white, westport, graphic arts school,
summer program, summer camp, summer classes, design degree,
graphic design degree, high school activity, art activity, westport
art program, ct art school, united states, usa, america, creative
workshop, professional development workshop" />

</head>
<body>

<!-- Navigation -->
   <ul id="nav">
     <li><a href="?page_id=5">Pre-College</li>
     <li><a href="?page_id=25">Workshops</li>
     <li><a href="?page_id=130">Video Library</li>
     <li><a href="?page_id=18">Art Colleges</li>
     <li><a href="?page_id=39">Resources</li>
     <li><a href="#">Online Classes</li>
   </ul>

<h1>MillerWhite School of Design - Graphic Design Classes,
Tutoring and Workshops**</h1>**

<h2>Pre-College Design Classes and Tutoring</h2>

<a href="http://millerwhiteschool.org/?page_id=6"><img src="http://
millerwhiteschool.org/images/mwsd_logo_black_small.gif"
align="left" border="0" title="graphic design for high school" /></
a><p>The MillerWhite School of Design offers advanced art and <a
href="?page_id=27">graphic design</a> coursework whose purpose
is to prepare <a href="?page_id=7">students</a> for <a href="?page_
id=5"><span class="blacklink">professional art education in college</
span></a>. </p>

<p><a href="?page_id=5">Learn about the design school »</a></p>

</body>

Internal SEO Factors

On-site SEO influencers can begin with the domain name or URL of the site. Finding the right domain name for a site can be difficult because so many names have already been taken, but choosing a completely arbitrary phrase could hurt a site's SEO value. Using a keyword in the URL can increase its relevance to certain topics. Also, the extension applied to the URL can effect its rank: .com and .org rank higher than other, less popular extensions like .me, .biz, or .us. The age of a domain can also play a role in a site's ranking. Similarly, keyword-rich page addresses can have a positive effect on SEO. For example, instead of naming a blog page using the date (www. example.com/2010/05/05/), the name should reflect the topic (www.example.com/widgets/widget_name/).

Developing a comprehensive SEO strategy means giving each page of a site an identity. This identity is formed and supported by key phrases or terms placed in strategic locations throughout the page. Not all key phrases will be used on every page—in fact, that's a common mistake. Instead, each page should focus on one or two key phrases to give provide the most impact for the spiders looking to confirm that a page is what it claims to be. Spiders validate a page by weighing or giving more importance to certain elements over others, making the location of keywords critical to the SEO success of a page.

Probably the most significant location for a key phrase is in the <title> tag for the page. This is the line of text that appears at the top of a user's browser window, above the address bar. Crawl-based search engines place a very high value on this text, as it's very likely to reflect the content of a page. Therefore, the content of the <title> tag should be clear and to the point. Repetitive or non-descriptive <title> tags have a negative effect, such as simply repeating the name of the site on every page title.

GigMasters.com is a site that allows users to book all types of entertainment. Their home page (right) contains text links to many categories of performers. These links combined with other internal SEO techniques consistently put GigMasters.com at the top of search listings.

Ultimately, SEO is about content—valuable content.

Navigation plays a significant role in SEO. Terms that appear in links are given higher value by spiders. Therefore, it's important that the main navigation be styled using "live" text—as opposed to images—when possible. Breadcrumbing, as discussed in Chapter 7, "Elements of Usability," is a great way to get keywords into links that appear on every page. Even the links within text play a part in SEO. When leading a user to another page, it's best to include keywords in the link ("Learn more about this widget" instead of just "Learn more"). Text-based site maps provide a useful tool for the user, but they also provide keyword-rich links for spiders. All of these keyword interlinks demonstrate to a search engine that the site, not just a single page, is rich with relevant content.

Ultimately, SEO is about content—valuable content. Each page of a site should contain at least some content, avoid landing pages or splash pages that simply lead a user to another page. (More on landing pages in a bit.) The content of each page should focus on a single key term or phrase and should be updated regularly. Syndicated content, or content that is being pulled from other sites via RSS (Real Simple Syndication), does not have significant SEO value; in fact, it can have a negative effect. Most importantly, content should be interesting to users. Users who value the content of a site generally tell others about it and even link to it from their site or through social media. These links and high traffic can have a profound effect on the rank of a page.

External SEO Factors

As discussed earlier in this chapter, search engines have shifted their ranking methods away from focusing solely on site content, to focusing on a site's popularity. Search engines assume that if a site has many visitors and is connected to other sites, it must have fresh and relevant content. In addition to simply looking at a site's traffic volume, search engines use a few additional factors.

First, they look at the inbound links (IBL) that a site has—links that people use to connect to a site from other sites. The more inbound links, the more likely it is that a site is trusted. In addition to simply counting the IBLs, spiders read text within the links, and if it matches the content of the page the ranking is boosted. The greatest value comes from two pages with similar content linking to each other. Similarly, but with a slightly lesser value, outbound links (OBL) to sites with relevant content can help with SEO. These links going out to other sites have lesser value because they can easily be manipulated by a Webmaster. The goal, however, is to demonstrate that the site exists within a community of sites with connections back and forth.

The second way to determine a site's popularity is by evaluating the click-through rate, or the number of times a link has been clicked by a user, on a search engine results page (SERP). This is where the meta description tag for a site comes into play. While Google and other search engines no longer use the content of the meta data to rank a page, they do use the meta description as the blurb below the link on their results pages. A well-written meta description can help entice users to click.

Finally, a site's popularity can be determined by its inclusion on directory sites. Since directories use knowledgeable human editors to evaluate the type and quality of content for a site, getting listed in a directory is a clear indication that a site lives up to its promise.

(Opposite) This diagram illustrates the top six external and internal SEO factors. SEO factors shift and change over time, but the goal of a Webmaster is to illustrate to a spider that a site is exactly what it's claiming to be.

A **comprehensive SEO strategy** targets high-value keywords with both an internal and external focus.

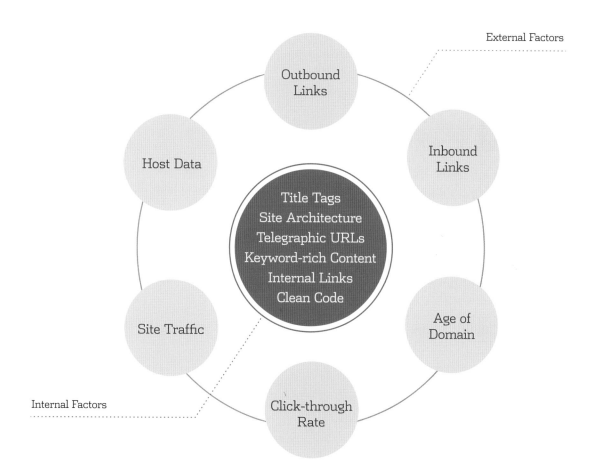

Paid Search

The concepts discussed to this point in this chapter produce what are known as organic search results—that is, the ranking of a site happened through the "natural" patterns and habits of users. There's another option to market and promote a site using search engines: paid search. It's called this because Webmasters pay to have their site listed on the search results page for specific terms. Paid search can be a valuable tool for marketers who are attempting to gain relevance in high-volume markets.

Paid search results appear at the top of most search results pages or on the right-hand side of the page. There is always some indication identifying paid search results, such as "Sponsored Links." This form of advertising can be sharply targeted to a specific segment of users, making it an attractive, relatively low-cost option for many clients. Pricing is usually based on the number of clicks an ad receives; this is why paid search is also called pay per click (PPC). Pricing is also based on the volume of the terms a campaign is targeting (the higher the search volume, the higher the price) as well as the position or "slot" that is desired—the top two slots cost more than the lower slots, for example.

The areas outlined in red are paid or sponsored search results. These links are paid for by advertisers targeting specific keywords—"SEO," in this case.

Paid search advertising can be **sharply targeted** to a specific segment of users, making it an attractive, relatively low-cost option for many clients.

Creating a paid search ad generally involves very little design— certainly none for the ad itself. Instead, ads are copy based and styled by the advertiser. A paid search ad consists of a headline and body copy that conform to a strict word count. This word count and the need to fit keywords into the text make writing effective paid search ads a unique art form. Copy for an ad also has the ability to be dynamically generated based on a user's search term. For example, a PPC ad campaign for Florida might have a headline that reads, "Looking for vacations in [Keyword]?" When a user searches "Orlando Vacation Packages," the paid search ad would read "Looking for vacations in Orlando?" This gives the user the impression that the content behind this link is extremely relevant to his or her needs.

Paid search ads can link to a page within the advertiser's site, but for greater tracking and conversion, they can also lead to what's called a *landing page.* Landing pages are specifically designed to maximize the return on investment (ROI) for paid search and advertising campaigns. Often, two or three landing pages will be created to test which messages and design treatments work best. Over time, the pages with lower conversion rates are eliminated, again maximizing the ROI. The topic of converting browsers into buyers is explored further in the next chapter.

CHAPTER 9

MARKETING & CONVERSION

This chapter explores various means of attracting users to a site, converting them to valuable customers, and maintaining a profitable relationship with them. From advertising and viral marketing to cross selling and up selling to email marketing, each phase of the customer cycle can have a large and lasting effect on the amount and value of users that come to a site.

S1
Design &
Typography

S2
Planning
& Usability

S3
Business
Effectiveness

Turning Browsers into Buyers

A Web site needs visitors in order for it to be seen as a success. Previous chapters have examined the methods of driving traffic through search engine optimization (SEO). SEO and search marketing sometimes aren't enough, especially when the client is looking to gain awareness among a specific target demographic for a product or service that's new or that fulfills a need that may not be obvious to a user. In these cases, a more proactive form of marketing is required—*Web marketing*. Web marketing is a multi-billion-dollar industry covering a wide spectrum of services, from banner advertising and paid sponsorships to more organic forms of advertising like viral and social marketing.

When implemented properly, SEO combined with effective Web marketing can drive large volumes of traffic to a site, but sheer numbers alone may not be good enough for a site to succeed long term. Most sites require the user to take an action, from signing up to be a member, to buying things, to viewing as many pages as possible, to help with advertising impressions. Therefore, it's important that marketing efforts drive *high-value visitors* to a site. High-value visitors are visitors that come to a Web site not by chance or just to browse, but with the purpose of completing the required action of the site. Finding high-value users is a matter of promoting a site through the proper channels to target the right type of user, and by creating a compelling campaign that appeals to the needs of that target demographic.

Web marketing is a multi-billion-dollar industry covering a wide spectrum of services from banner advertising and paid sponsorships to more organic forms of advertising like viral and social marketing.

Browsers can be converted into high-value visitors once they arrive at the site through on-site marketing techniques. Certainly the methods of clear design and planned usability play a role in converting browsers into buyers, but there are other tools that a design team can use to further increase the conversion rate of users. *Cross selling* is a means of telling a user, "If you like this, you might like that," and *up selling* is a means of telling a user, "This product is good, but that product will satisfy more of your needs." Both are effective ways to maximize the value of a user. Sharing mechanisms placed throughout the customer stream on a site can help spread the word about a site through word of mouth. This type of social sharing can be seen as significantly more trustworthy among potential users than banner advertising.

Once a customer has engaged with a client's brand by performing the required action on a site, the next step is to retain that customer. Retaining existing customers is vital for several reasons, but most important is the fact that it costs half as much to retain a customer than to attract a new one. Provided that an existing customer is happy with the experience, that person can help attract new customers by telling people about the experience and can even provide valuable feedback to the client about how to enhance the customer experience. Relationship marketing, which is used to communicate with existing customers, includes social marketing and email marketing. These elements help customers feel like they're on the inside and that they're appreciated.

Although entire books can and have been written on any one of these topics, this chapter gives an overview of the considerations a designer must make when attempting to add the most value for a client.

Banner Advertising

Creating an effective banner ad campaign involves many disciplines, from copywriting and design to media strategy, technology, and even psychology. Users have become accustomed to tuning out banner ads, so getting noticed takes knowing the right techniques for a specific audience. As with any form of advertising, Web banner advertising starts with the right media plan. A media plan is a strategy for determining where and when the banners will appear. These choices are made with several factors in mind, including the relevancy of the content on a site compared to the advertisement, the amount of traffic a site has, and the cost per click that a site offers.

Once in place, a media plan will dictate the types and sizes of interactive marketing units (IMU) needed for a campaign. The Interactive Advertising Bureau (IAB) has set standards for file size, dimension, and animation time. Included in the IAB standards are Universal Ad Package (UAP) sizes. UAP standards make it easier for companies to advertise, since advertisers only need to create a finite set of banner sizes that can be used across a wide range of sites. Universal Ad Package sizes (in pixels) include:

Leaderboard	728 x 90
Wide Skyscraper	160 x 600
Medium rectangle	300 x 250
Rectangle	180 x 150

A diagram showing the complete set of IAB IMUs is featured on the next spread.

IAB Ad Dimensions, File Sizes, and Animation Limits

Micro Bar
88 x 31, 10K, :15

Button 1
120 x 90, 20K, :15

Pop-Under
720 x 300, 40K, :15

Button 2
120 x 60, 20K, :15

Leaderboard
728 x 90, 40K, :15

Full Banner
468 x 60, 40K, :15

Half Banner
234 x 60, 30K, :15

Vertical Rectangle
240 x 400, 40K, :15

Square Pop-Up
250 x 250, 40K, :15

3:1 Rectangle
300 x 100, 40K, :15

Vertical Banner
120 x 240, 30K, :15

Square Button
125 x 125, 30K, :15

Half-Page Ad
300 x 600, 40K, :15

Wide Skyscraper
160 x 600, 40K, :15

Skyscraper
120 x 600, 40K, :15

Large Rectangle
336 x 280, 40K, :15

Medium Rectangle
300 x 250, 40K, :15

Rectangle
180 x 150, 40K, :15

A **click-through rate** is the number of people who've clicked on the banner and is expressed as a percentage of the number of people who have seen the ad, called **impressions**.

When creating a banner ad, a designer is looking to generate a high *click-through rate*. A click-through rate is the number of people who've clicked on the banner to go to the client's site. The click-through rate is expressed as a percentage of the number people who have seen the ad, called impressions. For example, if a banner is on a page where 25,000 people visit and 250 people click the banner, the click-through rate is one percent—an admirable rate for a site with this amount of traffic. This level of detailed statistical data is unique to Web marketing, and it enables a high level of control over a campaign. Often, a banner campaign will involve multiple versions of a banner and over time, high-performing banners can replace low-performing banners to maximize the click-through rate of each placement.

Banners present a unique design challenge because they usually exist in a cluttered environment. These banners for the Starbucks Love campaign are instantly recognizable across different sites and the design is consistent throughout the varying UAP sizes.

Detach and Distribute

Because click-through rates are often a very small percentage of the overall impressions a banner receives, marketers have begun thinking about and utilizing the space within a banner differently. A technique called detach and distribute *brings critical content and site features to the banner space, allowing users to engage with a brand without ever leaving the page they're on. Pioneered by Tom Beeby, creative director at the interactive marketing firm Beeby, Clark and Meyler, detach and distribute employs rich media to display a video, capture email addresses, or allow real-time social interactions, for example. This tactic of creating a mini-site within a site can be highly effective for increasing awareness of a product or service.*

These banners created for GE display both pre-recorded and live video content from GE.com and allow users to comment on the them in real time, right within the banner space.

Contextually relevant ads are ads that respond directly to the environment in which they are served.

Context is a critical aspect of all forms of advertising, but with Web advertising it can be taken to an even higher level. Contextually relevant ads are ads that respond directly to the environment in which they are served. This can mean something simple like placing an ad for fishing boats on a fishing Web site, but it can also be much more specific by drawing on data from the user including time-specific or location-specific placements. Contextually relevant banners have shown to be significantly more effective than one-size-fits-all banner campaigns.

Because of their unusual dimensions, shapes, file size limitations, and the need for immediate communication of a message, banner ads present a significant design challenge. The best advice a designer can heed is to put him- or herself in the shoes of the user and ask, "What would I respond to?" The answer is almost always a simple, relevant message, clearly stated with an obvious call to action. Animation can help grab attention and/or build a message within a limited space, but most sites do not permit repeating or looping animation since it can be very distracting to a user. Thus, the final frame of the banner should be designed and written in a way that all the critical information appears. The call to action, which is a sentence with a verb (*learn, click, try,* etc.) inviting the user to do something, should be clear—perhaps encased in a button-like object—and should directly relate to the content of the page the user is taken to after clicking the banner.

These banners from Apple Computer seem like ordinary ad placements, but there's a twist—the banners are synced with one another, making it possible for them to work together. In the ad seen here, Mac and PC are reacting to the leaderboard banner, which states that Apple is number one in customer experience, while the men in the seemingly unrelated "hair replacement" ad chime in to the conversation.

These amusing and engaging ads were awarded a Webby, one of the highest honors an online campaign can receive.

These ads for MySpace (top) and Pringles (left) use humor to engage the user and convey a brand message. This Pringles ad has received multiple accolades for its innovative use of adverting space. The ad continues seemingly forever with mundane conversation as part of Pringles' "Over Sharing" campaign.

Getting a user to engage with a
banner ad means getting a user to
engage with a client's brand.

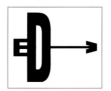

*(Above) This single banner for Zippo lighters
appears to be two banners, where the gentleman
in the upper banner is being heated up by the
lighter in the lower banner.*
*(Left) These banners for the Toyata Prius invite
users to draw on the banner. This action triggers
an animation that explains a feature of the car.*

*This interactive banner from Lotus Notes collaboration software invited
users to collaborate by manipulating the letters of the word "IDEA"
into various pictographs. Each user interacting with the ad would be
responsible for shaping a single letter.*

Rich media banners can be effective in grabbing a user's attention, but they can also be costly to produce and place making them suitable for a limited number of clients.

In addition to standard ad units, there are third-party solutions, such as EyeWonder and EyeBlaster (Media Mind), which provide a variety of rich media expandable banners. These banners include a wide range of interactive experiences from a simple expanding banner, to banners that communicate with one another, to page takeovers or roadblocks where the entire Web page is consumed with an ad. These banners can be effective in grabbing a user's attention, but they can also be costly to produce and place—so they're most suitable to a small number of clients who have large online advertising budgets.

These rich media banners for McDonald's completely take over the Web page. The top image is known as a "peel-back" ad, where the page can be turned like a page of a book to reveal an advertising message. The bottom ad is an expandable banner featuring characters that dance across the screen.

(Top) This ad for Tostitos includes two standard placements, a leaderboard, and big box, and also the background "skin," which visually relates to the ads.

(Bottom left) This ad for Sony features an expandable video player. The player expands over the page content, making the video larger.

(Bottom right) This video game ad consists of a leaderboard that expands with a graphic and a video, as well as the big box ad along the right side.

Viral Marketing

Viral marketing gets its name from the way a virus spreads rapidly and "infects" a population organically. Viral marketing works because such pieces provide some sort of entertainment value beyond the thousands of ordinary advertising messages consumers are bombarded with on a daily basis. Successful viral pieces hit on a universal concept—humor, fear, sex—and at first may not appear to be marketing pieces at all. Branding is usually subtle, or in some cases nonexistent. Because consumers are so overloaded with advertising messages, they're also very suspicious, which makes viral marketing difficult—very difficult, in fact.

Elf Yourself from OfficeMax allowed users to place family members' faces on dancing elves.

If a piece of marketing "goes viral," the impact can be profound. An early example of successful viral marketing was for the film *The Blair Witch Project.* Instead of standard big-budget TV and print ads, the producers released short clips of the film on the Internet. The clips were hauntingly scary, and the supporting Web site blurred

the lines between what was real and what was part of the movie. The film cost $350,000 to create and market, but grossed nearly $250 million at the box office—the highest profit-to-cost ratio of any film in history.

Have a break, have a Jesus Kit-Kat

Easter is time for Easter Bunny potato chips and Jesus sightings, and the latest is a doozy: Jesus has been spotted in a Kit-Kat.

The Kit-Kat hails from the Netherlands, where the story is a little Google Translate sketchy. Here's what I managed to pull out (original link/ translated)

Viral marketing doesn't have to be high-tech or high budget. This viral campaign from Kit Kat started with a photo and an email about seeing the face of Jesus. It quickly spread around the Internet, carrying with it the Kit-Kat messaging.

The phrase "viral marketing" may be relatively new, but the concept isn't. *Guerilla marketing*, popular in the 1990s, involved tactics such as spray-painting company logos as if by street artists to get people talking and to gain credibility among an urban demographic. Even political propaganda or rumor spreading can be considered a form of viral marketing.

Burger King and their interactive agency Crispin, Porter + Bogusky have a long history of creating viral content. Seen here is the subservient chicken who would do anything (really anything) the user typed into the field. Also seen here is The Simpsons Movie tie-in, Simpsonize Yourself. This Flash application allowed users to create Simpsons versions of themselves.

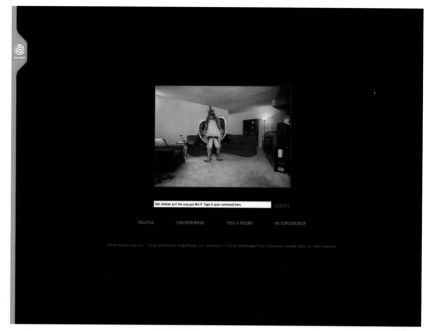

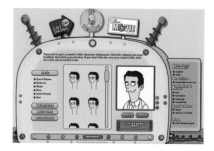

Brief History of Viral Videos

2000
John West Salmon

One of the earliest viral videos was this amusing TV spot for John West Salmon. Styled like a nature documentary complete with narration, the video quickly turns into an outrageous kung fu fight between a fisherman and a bear.

2001
BMW Films

Traditionally, companies try to have their products placed in high-budget films. In this example, BMW placed a high-budget film in their advertising. This glossy series of viral films was directed by David Fincher and Guy Richie and starred actors such as Don Cheadle, Clive Owen, and even Madonna.

2002
Agent Provocateur

This over-the-top viral video features Australian actress and singer Kylie Minogue riding a mechanical bull in Agent Provocateur lingerie. What started as a Super Bowl ad became a wildly popular Web video—especially among the male audience.

2006
DOVE

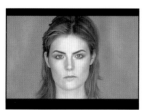

As part of Dove's "Real Beauty" campaign, this viral video titled "Evolution" looks at the transformation of a model from makeup to lighting to retouching using time-lapse photography. The message to young women was as powerful as the visual.

2006
HERE IT GOES AGAIN

Take six treadmills, four hipster musicians, and one infections song and get this low-budget, ingenious, and fun viral video. This video is proof that viral marketing is more about ideas than big budgets.

2007
GUITARMASTERPRO.NET

This extremely unassuming video featuring a 21-year-old guitar player playing Pachelbel's Canon received over 60 million views on YouTube. The video for a guitar lesson site relied completely on the talent of the subject—and it worked.

Social Marketing

Social marketing is similar to viral marketing in that it spreads organically through word of mouth—but social marketing usually involves a direct benefit to the user. Think of it this way: Viral marketing is a person going to a party with a cold and spreading it to the other partygoers; social marketing is a person going to a party with good news and actively telling as many people as he or she can.

Social marketing is used as much to get new customers as it is to retain existing customers. Building a social relationship with a customer by inviting them to be a friend on Facebook, for example, enables client organizations to market to these consumers in a new way. Offering coupons or exclusive deals can make consumers feel as if they're part of a brand and therefore will be more likely to spread positive information about a brand to their social network. These types of seemingly unaided endorsements have a profound ability to influence consumer opinion—so much so that companies are continually trying to blur the lines between "friends" and brands.

Social media isn't about fancy design; it's about engaging consumers on a different level than other forms of marketing. Social marketing is a conversation with the customer that makes the customer feel welcome and part of the client's company, as these examples illustrate.

Ben and Jerry's and JetBlue, whose Facebook and Twitter pages are seen here, respectively, do an excellent job extending their brand images with social media. This is in part because these brands already had a conversational relationship with their customers.

Viral marketing is a person going to a party with a cold and spreading it to the other partygoers; **social marketing** is a person going to a party with good news and actively telling as many people as he or she can.

Social marketing doesn't necessarily involve social networking sites. This delightfully social campaign called Save our Sounds allows users to upload a sound from where they live. The goal, says the creator, is to create a sound map of the world.

Honda Motors exploits the popularity of their brand with this clever social media campaign. Their claim is that everyone knows someone who loves a Honda. Using Facebook to make connections among users, this campaign quickly illustrated the popularity of Honda's vehicles.

Perhaps the most famous and certainly one of the earliest social/viral campaigns was this one from Burger King. The Whopper Sacrifice called upon Facebook users to "sacrifice" a few of their friends for a free hamburger. The campaign was extremely successful; however, it violated a rule on Facebook that bans telling friends when they've been defriended. Because of this, the campaign was ended but its impact lives on.

Getting a user to take action involves the right products, promotion, pricing, and placement—**the four P's of marketing**.

On-Site Marketing

Once a user has found a site, it's important to the client that the value is maximized. Clients want to get the most out of each visitor, and this can mean different things for different sites—from becoming a member to filling a shopping cart with products to buy. Getting a user to take this action can take more than clear navigation, well-planned usability, and effective design; as discussed in previous chapters, it also involves the right products, promotion, pricing, and placement—the four P's of marketing.

Having the right product development and pricing strategy is largely the responsibility of the client, and is usually determined prior to starting a Web project. Promoting and placing these products, however, can be the job of the Web project team. Promotion is a means of giving information about a product that piques the interest of the user. It's the job of an effective marketer to highlight important features of a product or service and clearly differentiate it from the competition. The Web offers a variety of ways to promote a product or service, from photo galleries and slideshows to highly interactive product showcases.

The product display on MarieCatribs.com is not only user friendly but client friendly as well. The photography and clean layout make accessing the products easy and inviting, which can lead to more sales and higher profits for the client.

JaqkCellars.com does a magnificent job displaying their products in a way that enhances their appeal. The product pages are simple, with a single focal point: the product. Flash is used to provide a 360-degree spinning view of the bottle. The dark "ADD TO CART" buttons stand out from the page, making it easy for the user to enter the buying process.

To **cross sell** is to recommend other products to a user based on his or her interest in a particular item.

The other P of on-site marketing is placement, which gives the user access to the product outside the context of the standard product or catalog page. Placement is the association of a product or service to content or other products or services. On a site that has health information and also sells health products, for example, an article about sprained ankles might be accompanied by a product placement of ankle braces for sale in the store.

Cross selling is a form of placement. Online retailers understanding that if a user is in the mood to buy one item, he or she is more easily persuaded into purchasing more items. This is where cross selling comes in. To cross sell is to recommend other products to a user based on his or her interest in a particular item. Cross selling associations can be done one of two ways: by the client linking products that relate to each other functionally—e.g., if you buy this Apple computer you might want this Apple mouse—and it can also be done with purchase history where users make the associations with their buying patterns—e.g. "Users who bought this item also bought..."

Up selling is similar to cross selling, except the goal is to get the customer to buy more expensive items or services. An effective way to up sell is through the use of a features chart. Features charts show side-by-side comparisons of one product to another, highlighting the benefits of purchasing the higher-priced item.

The items along the left side of this page from MeAndMommyToBe.com are related to the main product in some way and likely to be purchased at the same time.

Both TommyBahama.com and JPeterman.com cross sell their garments by offering additional items of a similar style on the product pages.

PotteryBarn.com offers a variety of selling tools on their product pages—from items in a set and related items to customer ratings and reviews.

Email Marketing

The site has been found and the sale made, but the customer cycle has one more component to close the loop: relationship building. Building a relationship with a user-turned-customer by regularly communicating with the person can be extremely valuable to a client. Repeat customers not only cost less than new customers, but they are likely to tell their friends about the product or service, which breeds new customers. One of the most effective ways to maintain a relationship with a customer is through email marketing. Email marketing "pushes" information about the client's product or service to the customer. Relationship marketing can take the form of a newsletter, where product information is accompanied by information that's valuable to the user.

There are strict laws governing the use of email marketing that designers and their clients should be aware of. Failure to comply with the laws contained in the CAN-SPAM Act can bring stiff fines to a client. The CAN-SPAM Act dictates the following guidelines for email marketing:

- Don't use false or misleading header information ("From," "Reply to")
- Don't use deceptive subject lines
- Identify the message as an ad
- Tell recipients where you're located
- Tell recipients how to opt out of receiving future emails
- Honor opt-out requests promptly
- Monitor what others are doing on your behalf

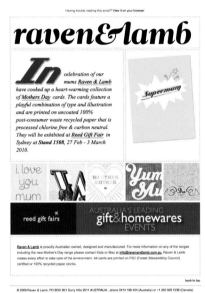

Source: http://www.ftc.gov/bcp/edu/pubs/business/ecommerce/bus61.shtm

mucca design

Newsletter n.6
May 2010

With birdsong filling the air and tender blooms rising to greet the sun, it can only mean one thing: they must be hailing the long-awaited arrival of... the new Mucca website! We've been working hard all winter to launch Mucca 3.0, so follow the frolicking lambs to mucca.com, and discover what's been keeping us from our usual newsletter release. Happy Spring!

ART WORLD HEAVYWEIGHTS

We are excited to announce that we recently partnered with Gagosian Gallery to promote two of their latest exhibition identities. We have enjoyed collaborating with the gallery on campaigns for two very different artists: Philip Taaffe and Pablo Picasso.

The Philip Taaffe exhibition is comprised of mesmerizing new paintings with a psychedelic streak, and the Pablo Picasso exhibit, Experiments in Linogravure, features expressive linocuts created between 1959 and 1963. For each show, we created a luxurious, collectible hardbound catalog and a range of promotional materials.

DESIGNING FOR OUR IDOLS

Imagine being asked to cook a meal for James Beard and Julia Child, and you'll understand the challenge we faced when the AIGA asked us to design a program for their 2009 Design Legends Gala, celebrating the lifetime achievement of selected design world luminaries. Because we are type nerds, we used only custom, unreleased typefaces, ensuring an evening of mystified guessing by our esteemed peers. Happily, this pressure cooker assignment resulted in a successful piece, although we did encounter some resistance from a certain champion of Helvetica: "There are too many typefaces, I honestly find it confusing..." —Massimo Vignelli

FOOD FOR THOUGHT

Thanks to Karen Waltuck of Chanterelle Restaurant, we had a gratifying opportunity to work pro bono with The Cooke Center for Learning and Development, a non-profit organization that benefits kids with special needs. We created an identity for their annual spring gala fundraiser that brings together world-renowned chefs for an evening of food and goodwill.

Novum

German graphic design magazine, Novum, featured us as "Italian magic" in NY. Ta da!

Matteo + the AIGA

Don't miss Matteo speaking in Denver on May 5th. Let's hope the altitude doesn't go to his head.

Type Forecast

Discover the future of fonts, as Matteo moderates the AIGA's May 14th Fresh Dialog talk

muccadesign.com   568 Broadway, Suite 504, New York, NY 10012   phone: +1 212 965 9821   fax: +1 212 625 9153

These email templates from Rave & Lamb (left) and Mucca Design (right) illustrate a simple elegance that's required for email designs. Because of the restrictions of mail browsers to display HTML and the need for immediate communication, email templates must focus on simplicity and clear hierarchy.

The **subject line** of an email acts as a headline and can play a pivotal role in the success of an email campaign.

Designing an email template presents another set of unique design challenges for Web designers. This is because email clients (Outlook, MacMail, etc.) are far less sophisticated in their ability to display HTML than Web browsers are. For example, the standard width of an email is 600 pixels, as opposed to 990 for a Web site. File sizes matter, since the user hasn't necessarily requested to see the content of the email. Emails with long load times tend to get deleted and go unread. Emails are primarily limited to HTML and standard image formats—jpg, gif—Flash, JavaScript, and movie formats are currently unsupported by most email clients. Linking to external files for styling, for example, is also unsupported. Therefore CSS coding must be done "in-line" meaning in the individual tags for each HTML element.

The subject line of an email acts as a headline and can play a pivotal role in the success of an email. Subject lines should speak specifically to the subject of the email with clarity and brevity. Often, as with online banner advertising, multiple subject lines are tested for efficacy, and subject lines with higher open rates can replace more poorly performing lines to maximize the success of an email. Email layouts require simplicity even more so than Web pages because they are often scanned by the user. When creating an email, a designer should consider the primary goal of the email and focus the design on that element by creating a clear hierarchy of information. Emails should include at least some HTML-based text because some email clients and mobile devices only display the text of an email. The footer of an email, by law, needs to indicate who the email was sent to, who it was sent by, and a means for the user to opt out from receiving future emails.

These email templates illustrate how even within the constraints of email browsers the design can still be an extension of a client's brand, increasing brand recognition among users.

 Scott & Nix [Forward to a Friend]

Newsletter
Fishing with Kids
May 2010

Take a Child Fishing

THE SUNFISH
Tips for a successful first outing with your young angler

1. Keep the trip short. **2.** Catch a fish.

3. Have a sandwich and a juice box on hand for when the fishing's done.

Pick a warm day, and take your youngster to a dock on a pond or a lake for sunfish. Beginnings are a delicate thing, and no one likes to get skunked, especially kids.

Trout and bass can be finicky and elusive. Sunfish are eager feeders and plentiful in most freshwater lakes.

Feel free to share our newsletter with your friends. Click here to forward it to someone you know.

The Quarry

It's nice to know what you're catching and sunfishes are an amazingly diverse group. All are members of the large Centrarchidae family, which includes freshwater basses, crappies, bluegill, pumpkinseed, and others. In all, there are 27 species and all are native to North America. The classic group of sunfishes, a.k.a. panfishes, are all included on the Sunfishes of North America wall poster.

SPECIES INCLUDE:

pumpkinseed · redear sunfish · flier
bluegill · dollar sunfish · shadow bass
spotted sunfish · warmouth · Ozark bass
orangespotted sunfish · redbreast sunfish · black crappie
redspotted sunfish · green sunfish · white crappie
longear sunfish · rock bass

SUNFISHES OF NORTH AMERICA

The Sunfish of North America poster is illustrated by the amazing Joe Tomelleri. You can see more of his illustrations on posters at our site, and at his website, americanfishes.com.

The Gear

The Pole
Any light-weight fishing pole will do with a small reel and some 2- to 4-pound test line. You don't even really need a reel. This might be the time to use that old cane pole in the garage or to cut a branch from a willow and make one yourself.

The Hook and Knot
Use a number 6 hook, tied on the line using a clinch knot:

The Bobber
A simple one-inch adjustable bobber will do the trick. Place the bobber 18 inches above the hook.

The Bait
Earthworms (cut in small portions) are the traditional bait. You can also use live crickets (easy to catch in the cool of the morning), bits of soft pet food, small balls of white bread, mealworms, or even uncooked bacon. Sunnies will bite at just about anything.

Catching sunnies couldn't be easier and along the way, you can patiently explain some safety rules about hooks and how to gently release the fish back into the water. You will be rewarded with a very happy child and perhaps even the beginnings of a life-long angler.

The Technique

Toss the baited hook and bobber toward the shore or near the protective cover of the dock. Let it splash down and wait three seconds (counting it out with your child). Reel or pull the bobber back toward you, 12 inches, and let it sit. Keep an eye on it. It won't take long for the nibbling to begin. When the bobber goes under, give a slight tug to set the hook, and then slowly reel it in. Don't yank too hard, lest your child be unceremoniously introduced to a flying fish! If the bobber is just bobbing and not going under, try a smaller bit of bait.

Fish Stories

Before you get home, be sure to work out your story together. How big was the fish? How many did you catch? Fish stories are an integral part of the experience, and while we don't advocate fibbing, a little hyperbole won't hurt.

—Scott & Nix

[Forward to a Friend] [Subscribe to Our Newsletter] [Contact Us]

CHAPTER 10

ANALYSIS

The final component of the Web design cycle is analysis. While
all forms of marketing are analyzed and optimized, no form
of marketing or design can be analyzed with the immediacy,
accuracy, and depth that Web marketing can. What used to
take weeks or months to collect and report now happens in real
time. This immediacy allows marketers and designers to make
calculated adjustments that improve the overall performance of
their online assets. From banner campaigns to site design and
usability, to email campaigns and social media, all aspects of user
activity and brand engagement can be tracked at a granular level.

S1
Design &
Typography

S2
Planning
& Usability

S3
Business
Effectiveness

Analysis

249

Closing the Loop

Web site statistics have come a long way from the counters that used to be seen at the bottom of Web pages. Those could only tell the Webmaster the number of people who visited the site. Today, almost any action by a user can be tracked and analyzed—from where the visitor came; what words were used to search and find a site; how long the visitor was on a site; how many pages were visited—right down to if the person converted into a paying customer. Beyond the behavioral statistics, demographic information such as geographic location, browser type, OS, and connection speed can also be collected. Such statistics provide a marketing and design team with a wealth of useful information for optimizing site and campaign performance.

Analytical data can help remove a level of subjectivity from the creative process by providing qualitative data that supports one direction over another. Unfortunately, this data may not always support the designer's position. Web designers must be open to the notion that their designs will need to change and shift based on the habits and feedback of their users. What works for an audience today may be different next year, next month, or even next week. Technology evolves, users evolve, and environments evolve, making the Web and Web design more about progress and adaptability than permanence or even the level of perfection that comes with other forms of design.

The most common method of collecting statistical data is with Google Analytics, a free yet remarkably robust tracking system provided by Google.com. There are other free services, such as Piwik, which is a PHP-based open source system with many of the same features as Google Analytics. There are paid services, like WebTrends, that help their clients interpret their site statistics with reports and consulting.

These counter icons are what Webmasters once used to track users who came to a site.

In the case of Web design, very often **progress** is more important than **perfection.**

This chapter examines various data points that Google Analytics reports on and how they can affect the decisions a designer makes. Each data point can provide valuable information, but the full potential of Web analysis comes when the statistics are used in concert with one another. Focusing too heavily on any single statistic can mislead a designer. Combining key statistics can give a more complete picture of the strengths and weaknesses of a site. For example, if a site has a low average time on site statistic, this can be either a positive or a negative—but it's difficult to tell with this statistic alone. If the low average time on site is combined with a high *bounce rate* (the percentage of people who leave after only viewing the home page), then there could be an issue with engaging people in the site content. If, however, the low average time on site statistic is combined with a high number of pages viewed and the exit page leads a user to an online retailer to buy the product, for example, this would mean the site is working quite effectively in driving users to purchase.

What follows are brief explanations of various key statistics that Google Analytics reports on.

This is the Visitors Overview page of Google Analytics. By carefully tracking and cross-referencing the information displayed here, a designer can learn critical information about the habits of the users of a site and possibly inform future design decisions.

User Data

These data points tell a Webmaster or designer what he or she needs to know about the users who visit a site. From the number of visits to the capabilities of the user's technology, understanding the user is critical to the success of a Web site project.

VISITS

This indicates the total number of visitors to a site. It includes new and returning visitors and is an indication of the success or failure of an SEO strategy or marketing campaign. The number of visits can be an overrated statistic in that it's not an indication of the value of the visitors in terms of how long they spent on the site or what percentage are returning because they liked the experience. Like most of the statistics in this chapter, the analyst needs to cross-reference the visits with other statistics to really understand its value.

The term *visits* is sometimes confused with hits, but the two terms are not synonymous. A *hit* is a reference to the retrieval of a page asset from a server. For example, if a single user goes to a page with eight images and an external CSS file, each image plus the page and the CSS file will count as a hit—in this case, ten hits—but the page will have gotten only one visit. While hits have importance to an IT staff, designers and marketers should avoid citing hits as an indicator of a site's popularity as it can represent a misleading and inflated view of site statistics.

ABSOLUTE UNIQUE VISITORS

Absolute unique visitors are visitors visiting a site for the very first time. Analytical reporting takes place over a specific time period; the default in Google Analytics is the past thirty days, but the range can be set for any length of time. Absolute unique visitors are not only visiting a site for the first time during the selected time period, but visiting the site for the first time ever. This can be helpful in understanding the success of a marketing campaign whose goal is to build awareness among a new target audience.

NEW VISITS

New Versus Returning Visits is sometime confused with absolute unique visitors, but there's a slight difference. New visits are visits to a site by users who've visited the site prior to the time range being analyzed, but it's their first time back during that time period. This data point is expressed as a percentage—56% indicates fifty-six percent of the visitors were new during the time period, and by inference, for example, forty-four percent had visited the site more than once during the time period.

Visits ▾

Visits
1 ▨▨▨▨▨▨ 4,506

12,331 visits came from 119 countries/territories

Detail Level: City | Country/Territory | Sub Continent Region | Continent   Dimension: None ▾

BROWSER CAPABILITIES

The *Browser Capabilities* statistic shows both the number and percentage of browser types and technologies used by the visitors of a site. Understanding the capabilities of the majority of the users of a site is essential for designing and building the right experience for them. Included under browser capabilities is not only the browser type (Safari, Firefox, Internet Explorer, Chrome, etc.) but also operating system; screen resolution and colors; Flash version; and Java support. Each of these points paints a picture of the target users' capabilities and informs decisions made surrounding the types of technology used for a Web site.

NETWORK PROPERTIES

This feature indicates the service providers and hostnames of the users, but the most relevant data point for designers is the connection speed. Common connections speeds include (from fastest to slowest) T1, DSL, cable, ISDN, and dialup. Knowing the connection speed of the majority of the users of a site is critical to designing the right experience. The slower the connection speed, the lower the tolerance will likely be for graphics, imagery, and media assets that take time to download.

MOBILE

Increasingly, sites are being viewed using mobile devices, such as iPhones. This section of Google Analytics displays both the devices and the carriers of a site's mobile users. If a large number of visitors frequent a site via mobile devices, it may warrant a mobile version of the site.

MAP OVERLAY

Understanding the geographic location of the visitors to a site is can play a role in informing the direction of a site. The *Map Overlay* feature of Google Analytics shows the countries where users have visited a site. The intensity of the color indicates the number of visitors—the darker the green, the more visitors. This allows Web content developers to gear the content of a site in a way that is relevant to the users in the countries visiting the site.

LANGUAGES

Similar to the map overlay, the *Languages* report can help a client understand the needs of the actual demographic, which can be different from the target demographic. Languages are determined by the users' computer preferences and are reported in Google Analytics.

The image above shows the map overlay feature in Google Analytics. The darker the green, the more visitors that have come to a site from that country.

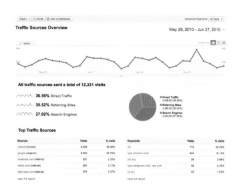

Source Data

Once there's an understanding of the user, it's important to know how the user is finding a site. Source data plays a critical role in search engine optimization as well as marketing, because it gives a Webmaster the knowledge of how users may have become aware of a site.

TRAFFIC SOURCES

Understanding the source of the visitor traffic to a site is critical for optimizing SEO and marketing efforts. Google Analytics' *All Traffic Sources* report shows the sources of traffic, including direct, search engines, and referring sites. The direct traffic number indicates users who simply typed the URL into their Web browsers. This can indicate a number of things to a marketing team, including whether the user saw a Web address in a non-online advertising campaign like print, radio, or TV.

REFERRING SITES

The *Referring Sites* tab shows sites that visitors used to link to the site being analyzed. This data is extremely valuable from an SEO perspective. The more sites that link to the subject site, the higher that site will rank for certain terms. Google Analytics displays the referring sites and the number of visitors that came from that site. By clicking on a site in the list, one can see the specific page the link came from.

SEARCH ENGINES

The *Search Engine* report shows the search engines that visitors used to search and find the subject site. This report can play an important role in determining the right sites for a search marketing campaign, as marketers want to advertise in the places where their target audience will see them.

KEYWORDS

The *Keywords* report is one of the most essential tools for understanding how users are finding a site. It shows a list of the words that visitors used to search for and link to a site. This can help validate or disprove an SEO keyterm strategy by showing the project team what words are actually being used to find a site. If the report matches the list of keywords the site targeted, the SEO strategy is a success. If they don't match, however, one of two things must occur. The team could look at the list and adjust it if there's an indication that the list misjudged what users were after; more likely, the implementation of the SEO tactics could be reexamined and improvements made to increase the performance of the original keyword list.

The visual above shows the traffic source information. The pie chart indicates the three types of traffic sources: direct traffic, referring sites, and search engines.

Content Data

The final step in understanding analytical data is looking at what users are doing on a site. When combined, stats like landing pages, time on site, pageviews, and exit pages can give a clear view of how users are using a site.

The content overview page on Google Analytics, pictured above, shows the pageviews, unique views, and bounce rates for a site.

PAGEVIEWS

Pageviews is as simple as the name implies— the number of pages viewed by visitors to a site. Pageviews is a broad statistic—and, like total visits, can be somewhat misleading. For example, if a user reloads a page, that can count as a second pageview. Similarly, if a user browses from a page to another page, then back to the original, that too will count as two pageviews for the original page.

AVERAGE PAGEVIEWS

Average Pageviews is the result of the number of pageviews divided by the number of visits on a given day. This can be helpful in showing trends from day to day. Whereas *Pageviews* refers to the total number of pages viewed over the entire time period, *Average Pageviews* refers to the number of pages the average visitor viewed on a single day, then tracked over time.

BOUNCE RATE

The *Bounce Rate* is usually given as a percentage and indicates the percentage of people who left a site after visiting only a single landing page—the home page, for example. Generally, a high bounce rate is not a good thing. It can indicate that information is difficult to navigate, the traffic sources are misleading, or the content is of poor quality. In some rare cases a high bounce rate is acceptable. For example, if a landing page effectively targets a specific keyword, a user may arrive at the page, get all the information needed, and then perhaps leave by clicking on a banner ad placed on the page. Despite going to only one page, that user might have a favorable opinion of the site and the client-generated revenue with the ad click. More often, however, a high bounce rate is not good.

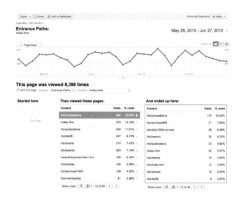

Average Time on Site

Average Time On Site is, as the name implies, the average length of time users spend on a site. This statistic is calculated by subtracting the difference in time between the first and the last pageview. As a result, it can be somewhat inaccurate in terms of the exact amount of time users are spending on a site. If the last page of the visit involves a time-consuming task—which is usually the case if a user is watching a video or reading an article—then the time on site would actually be much longer. Designers and Webmasters are looking for trends, rather than specific time, when analyzing the time on site statistics.

Top Landing Pages

The *Top Landing Pages* are the pages that visitors are using to enter a site. Therefore, this data can be critical to a designer's decision-making process. It's important for designers to understand that not all visitors will be "landing" or arriving at the home page. With SEO and referring links, almost any page of the site can be a landing page. Designers need to provide the same type of marketing, usability, and accessibility on landing pages as they do on the home page.

Top Content

Top Content shows the pages on a site that were most viewed by visitors. This statistic shows the specific pages that were viewed and how many times they were viewed. This report also displays the average time users spent on each page, the bounce rate for each page, and the percentage of users who exited on a specific page. This can be helpful in gaining an understanding of what users want from a site. It can also help to show prospective advertisers where users are spending the most time when planning advertising sales.

Top Exit Pages

Exit Pages are the last pages users viewed on a site. Users exit a site for various reasons—they've completed their task, or they clicked on an ad or link—or for less positive reasons, like they couldn't find what they were looking for or couldn't complete the required task. Together with landing pages and content statistics, exit page statistics complete the picture of how users arrive, what they do, and how they leave a site. Pages with unexpectedly high exit rates should be reexamined by the design team for usability issues that could cause users to leave the site prematurely.

The Entrance Path feature of Google Analytics shows where users entered a site and, based on that entry point, where they ended up.

INDEX